W9-BVJ-209

THE Overload Syndrome

LEARNING TO LIVE WITHIN YOUR LIMITS

RICHARD A. SWENSON, M.D.

NAVPRESS

BRINGING TRUTH TO LIFE

NavPress Publishing Group

P.O. Box 35001, Colorado Springs, Colorado 80935

The Navigators is an international Christian organization. Our mission is to reach, disciple, and equip people to know Christ and to make Him known through successive generations. We envision multitudes of diverse people in the United States and every other nation who have a passionate love for Christ, live a lifestyle of sharing Christ's love, and multiply spiritual laborers among those without Christ.

NavPress is the publishing ministry of The Navigators. NavPress publications help believers learn biblical truth and apply what they learn to their lives and ministries. Our mission is to stimulate spiritual formation among our readers.

Library of Congress Catalog Card Number: 98-17030
ISBN 1-57683-067-5
Cover photo by Neal Brown/Graphistock

Some of the anecdotal illustrations in this book are true to life and are included with the permission of the persons involved. All other illustrations are either composites of real situations or fictitious, and any resemblance to people living or dead is coincidental.

Unless otherwise identified, all Scripture quotations in this publication are taken from the *HOLY BIBLE: NEW INTERNATIONAL VERSION*© (NIV©). Copyright © 1973, 1978, 1984, International Bible Society. Used by permission of Zondervan Publishing House. The other versions used include *King James Version* (KJV). Copyright © 1909, 1917, copyright renewed 1937, 1945, Oxford University Press, New York, Inc., and *New American Standard Bible* (NASB). Copyright © 1960, 1962, 1963, 1968, 1971, The Lockman Foundation, La Habra, CA.

Swenson, Richard A.
    The overload syndrome: learning to live within your limits /
Richard Swenson.
        p.cm.
    Includes bibliographical references.
    ISBN 1-57683-067-5 (hardcover)
    1. Christian life. 2. Stress (Psychology)—Religious
aspects—Christianity. I. Title.
BV4501.2.S887 1998
248.4—dc21   98-17030
                                                                    CIP

Printed in the United States of America

1 2 3 4 5 6 7 8 9 10 11 12 13 14 / 05 04 03 02 01 00 99 98

Contents

To my wife, Linda, and
to our children, Adam and Matt

Daily, you make it all worthwhile.

Acknowledgments

Although much of my study and writing is done in "solitary confinement," scores of people rightfully deserve credit for significant contributions.

Don Steffen provided timely advice and a providential game-saving tackle. Don Simpson continues to inspire with his nobility. Bill and Gail Thedinga contributed helpful materials. The staff at several libraries—most prominently Dennis Olson and Lelah Lugo—lent valuable assistance. Ruth Swenson and Genevieve Wilson sent resources that fit perfectly into the text. Wilbur and Dan Hutchinson generously provided tapes.

The Bochmans, through their Hospitality House, provided a temporary sanctuary for in-depth work. Darlene Bochman once again demonstrated secretarial skills unsurpassed on this planet— the only person I have ever met who can finish transcribing before I finish dictating.

The NavPress staff has been gracious in encouragement, guidance, and resources. Terri Hibbard was patient and thorough in her editing, leaving the book better for her unflagging efforts.

My wife, Linda, helped more than I can recount. It would require another chapter to catalog her many contributions, including copy-editing, reading and research, handling administrative details and running errands, phoning and E-mailing, and so on, to say nothing of her nonstop affirmation. Adam and Matt contributed with their patience, and, of course, by simply being our children.

Jack and Diana Stimmel, Remy Diederich, Joanne Natwick, Joan Mecusker, Hector Cruz, Caroline Miller, Marcia Borgie, Warren and Karen Swenson, Becky Folkestad, Opal Harstad, Aggie and Tonya Wagner, as well as many other family and friends—all have contributed through both prayer and practical help along the way.

To each, please accept my heartfelt gratitude.

Introduction

Time to Rest, Space to Heal

Life in modern-day America is essentially devoid of time and space. Not the Star Trek kind. The sanity kind. The time and space that once existed in the lives of people who regularly lingered after dinner, helped the kids with homework, visited with the neighbors, sat on the lawn swing, went for long walks, dug in the garden, and always had a full night's sleep.

People are exhausted. Like the mother of four from LaGrange, Illinois, who said: "I'm so tired, my idea of a vacation is a trip to the dentist. I just can't wait to sit in that chair and relax."

People are stressed. Like the neurosurgeon who quit medicine to open a bagel shop. People are breaking the speed limit of life. Like the man who confessed: "I feel like a minnow in a flash flood."

People are overloaded. Like . . . me. Or at least I was. But that is the story of this book. If overload is sitting on our collective chests and blowing smoke in our faces, what can we do about it? Where is the pause button for the world?

We need more time. We need more space. We need more reserves. We need more buffer. We need, in short, more margin.

A FLAWED FORMULA FOR THE PERFECT LIFE

There was a point in my life when, of necessity, I decided to investigate a more margined way of living. Everything seemed out of control. I remember one day in particular—a Tuesday in 1982. I was finishing an evening meeting across town and beginning a migraine at the same time. Meanwhile back home, my wife, Linda, went for a late evening walk. Along the dark street, her crying could be in private.

My headache and Linda's crying were both manifestations of the same illness: overload. We were not only working, we were

11

overworking. We were not only committed, we were overcommitted. We were not only conscientious, we were overly conscientious. We were not only tired, we were exhausted.

Everything had become a burden: medicine and patients, caring and serving. How could so many good things bring such pain? We were not involved in anything that was bad—nothing unsuccessful, nothing selfish, nothing evil. We were meeting needs everywhere we turned.

Yet life was obviously out of control. Joy dried up and blew away. Buoyancy sank. Enthusiasm evaporated. Rest was a theoretical concept. My passion for medical practice shriveled to the size of a dehydrated pea.

Frankly, I was mystified. No one had taught me about this in medical school. Nor in residency. Nor in church. If fifteen years earlier I had written a formula for the perfect life—I had achieved it all. I had a prestigious career, a generous income, grateful patients, supportive colleagues, a great clinic, a brand new hospital, a wonderful town, a loving family, a vibrant church, and a growing faith.

But if we had such a perfect life, why was I getting all these headaches? Why was Linda crying? Why was it so hard to get out of bed in the morning? Why did I dread looking around the next corner?

If we had such a perfect life, why did we live so far from Utopia?

SIMPLE PLEASURES

At the same time, good friends of ours were going through a financial nightmare. Steve, who had started his own business, had an outstanding reputation and was well-liked by both employees and clients. Still, the economic realities of the early eighties—with sky-high inflation and equally high interest rates—had a strangle hold on his company. Our dear friends were actively being crushed by the resultant financial destitution.

One summer day—again, in 1982—my wife saw Steve and Lisa walking down the street hand-in-hand. She stopped to greet them, finding out they were on their way to buy a small ice cream cone. Two miles each way. Walk and talk. Total time: two hours. Total cost: fifty cents. It was the kind of date they could afford.

Linda was pleased to see them enjoying the weather and each other's company. Yet, at the same time, she couldn't help feeling a little envious. Oh, to have the time to walk and talk! To have the pleasure of an uninterrupted afternoon together. Why was it so hard to find the simple joys we knew when first married? Our world was like a pinball machine, and we were careening through life like unhappy electrons that had jumped their orbits. It was time to reconsider some basics.

AN EXAMPLE TO FOLLOW

Perhaps the turning point came when I decided to examine more closely the practice style of the Great Physician. How did Jesus care for people? He focused on the person standing in front of Him at the time. In my case, however, the person standing in front of me was often an obstacle to get around or over in order to get where I was going—even if that person was Linda or one of our two sons, Adam and Matt.

If Jesus had chosen to live in modern America instead of ancient Israel, how would He act? Would He have consulted a pocket calendar? Would He have worn a watch? Would He have carried a beeper? Can you imagine Him being paged out of the Last Supper?

When I look deeper at the life of Christ, I also notice that there is no indication He worked twenty-hour ministry days. He went to sleep each night without having healed every disease in Israel—and He apparently slept well. Neither did He minister to everybody who needed it. Neither did He visit or teach everybody who needed it. There were many needs that He simply chose not to meet. Even when Lazarus became sick, Jesus was shockingly slow to mobilize. I would have had a helicopter there in twenty minutes. But Jesus delayed for two days.

Is this to imply that He was lazy or didn't care? Of course not. But it is to imply that He understood what it meant to be human. Jesus was fully God and fully human, and His fully human side understood what it meant to have limits. Jesus understood what it meant to prioritize and to balance in light of those limits and how to focus on the truly important. We can learn a lesson from Jesus— it's okay to have limits. It is okay not to be all things to all people all of the time all by ourselves. At any given moment, the most important thing in life is the person standing in front of us.

When I finally learned these lessons about availability and prioritizing, life changed. For the first time in my life, I recognized the importance of leaving a margin. The more I understood the phenomenon of margin, the more I realized its importance. And the more I understood its importance, the more I yearned for its freedom in my own life.

Carefully, and even forcefully, Linda and I carved out margin in four areas: emotional energy, physical energy, time, and finances. As we did, ninety percent of our pain disappeared. Life came alive again. My passion for medicine returned in full force.

We remain busy, to be sure. But we are no longer chronically overloaded. We still serve, teach, and help with a full investment of passion and enthusiasm. But always within the context of limits.

REDESIGNING LIFE

I will never forget the evening when Linda and I, on our living room floor, decided it was time to make substantive changes. Together we took out a pad of paper and sat down before the fireplace. "Let's start by pretending everything in our lives is written on this paper," I suggested. "Every attitude, every activity, every belief, every influence.

"Then let's erase it all. Tear up the paper and throw it in the fire. Wipe the slate clean. Erase away all our beliefs, everything we have been taught by parents, friends, society, church. Remove all our hopes and dreams. Remove all our possessions. Nothing should remain. Then let's give the pencil to God and ask Him to redesign our lives by that which is fully and spiritually authentic."

It was an exciting evening. An exhilarating sense of freedom swept over us. As we wrestled control of our lives away from the world, we felt the elephant slipping off our backs. And as we turned and handed control over to God, no spiritualized elephant took its place. The Father, we instantly sensed, had in mind much more than our survival. It was an indescribable feeling.

Our redesigned life was simpler. That decision reduced our income significantly, but the freedom, the time, the rest, and the balance have been well worth it. We have never looked back.

Today, because of margin, I no longer dread getting up in the morning or looking around the next corner. Today, when I hang out the "Gone Fishing" sign on my door, I don't worry about the opinion of the world. Now, as I head down the road with my family, I know that the same God who invented both rest and relationship is wishing us a good catch.

MARGIN, LIMITS, AND OVERLOAD

Margin is the space that once existed between our load and our limits. Margin is the space between vitality and exhaustion. It is our breathing room, our reserves, our leeway. Margin is the opposite of overload, and therefore the antidote for that vexatious condition.

Yet overload has recently become the majority of American experience. Because of the rapidly changing conditions of modern living—largely due to progress always giving us more and more of everything faster and faster—we are exceeding our limits in scores of areas all at the same time. From activity overload to choice overload to debt overload to expectation overload to information overload to work overload, we are a piled-on, marginless society.

The contemporary American axiom is to *maximize everything*. We push the limits as far as possible. Then we push some more. This has become not only business dogma but also standard operating procedure for nearly every sociological experience. We spend ten percent more than we have—and it no longer matters if one is talking about time, energy, or money. We work hard, play hard, and crash hard.

For many of us, that once popular axiom is no longer working. It is time to consider replacing it with a new axiom: *leave a margin*. Most of us need some time in which to rest and some space in which to heal. Our relationships desperately need some margin in which to be revitalized.

LEAVING A MARGIN FOR ERROR

If you were flying from Minneapolis to Boston, would you leave just two minutes to change planes in Chicago? (I tried it once. Not recommended.) If you were going 65 miles per hour on the interstate, would you leave a mere two feet between you and the car ahead? If you were interviewing for an important job, would you show off your understanding of management principles by arriving "just in time"? Political observer Peggy Noonan comments, "I think the essential daily predicament of modern Americans is this: There is no margin for error anymore."[1]

To illustrate the practical importance of margin, let me relate a story. Several years ago, a medical colleague became engaged. Having taught this delightful young physician, I was pleased to receive an invitation to the wedding.

They were to be married on an August afternoon at 3:00 P.M. As our home is a half-hour from the church, at 2:25 P.M. I loaded my family into the car and headed east. By my calculations, we would have thirty minutes to get to the church, five minutes to find a pew, and zero minutes to waste. The organ would start, the bride would begin down the aisle. . . .

As planned, we arrived in the church parking lot at precisely 2:55 P.M. Perfect timing. So far, so good. There was only one problem. The parking lot was empty. Completely empty. Not as in *I'm early* empty, but as in *I've got the wrong church* empty. There were seventy other churches in the city, and I had five minutes to find the right one. Normally a good problem solver, I came quickly to a plan. Linda, too, had a plan. The trouble was her plan and my plan were not the same plan. And, of course, neither would get us to the church on time.

I am not an irritable person, and Linda is even less so. But I was irritable right then. It was hot, and I was starting to perspire. Linda and I exchanged conflicting suggestions for solving our dilemma and redeeming what was left of the wedding. Meanwhile our two delightful boys were in the back seat discussing how incompetent their parents were.

We finally found the church—but, of course, arrived twenty minutes late. Squeezing into a back pew, I had worked up an uncomfortable sweat. Somehow our anticipation of a delightful afternoon spent with friends celebrating the highlight of a life had not quite turned out as hoped.

We had left no margin for error. And we had paid the price.

BENEFITS VERSUS DRAWBACKS

Being marginless means that we are expended, depleted, and exhausted with no oasis in sight. Having margin, however, means that when we are drained, we have someplace to go for our healing. Many people, desperate for something other than their daily diet of stress and overload, yearn to regain margin in their lives.

The margined life has much to commend about it.

Joy

As a result of a very unscientific survey, I have noticed that people, in general, do not like being marginless. On the other hand, most people do like having margin. The vast majority of Americans simply do not enjoy living at one hundred and twenty percent all the time. Most of us would jump at the chance to slow down and give joy an opportunity to gain a new foothold.

Service

Margin permits service to the needs of others. Research demonstrates that people involved in helping others are themselves healthier. But who has time to serve? When Colin Powell convened the Volunteerism Summit in Philadelphia, *USA Today* headlined: "Overstressed, Overworked: Who Has Time to Volunteer?" The modern marginless lifestyle is toxic to service.

Health

Margin is health enhancing. Our bodies are enormously self-correcting. But they must be given a chance. Margin allows both the soma and the psyche a chance to heal. It gives our immunological equilibrium a chance to right itself. Even the best crew can't fix a race car when it is going 200 miles per hour. Neither can our bodies perform needed repairs in the midst of a hyperliving lifestyle.

Relationships

Margin nourishes the relationships most important to us. It allows time to communicate and grants space in which to reach out. My advice: Don't trust the vitality of your relationships to the normal flow of culture, because right now, culture isn't helping.

Availability

Margin allows availability for the purposes of God. When God taps us on the shoulder and asks us to do something, He doesn't expect to get a busy signal. "In the spiritual life," explains theologian Henri Nouwen, "the word discipline means 'the effort to create some space in which God can act.' Discipline means to prevent everything in your life from being filled up. Discipline means that somewhere you're not occupied, and certainly not preoccupied. In the spiritual life, discipline means to create that space in which something can happen that you hadn't planned or counted on."[2]

Without margin, we are self-protective, painfully uninterested in an opportunity to serve our neighbor. Without margin, we tread water and hang on by our fingernails, trying to survive another day. Without margin, we are chronically exhausted, chronically late, chronically rushed. Without margin, we are overloaded.

Margin, on the other hand, tells us to guard our reserves. Create buffers and fortify them. Carve out some space between our load and our limits. Don't be chronically overloaded, overcommitted, and overwhelmed. Give ourselves space to rest, room to breathe, freedom to move, time to adapt, and money to spare. Only then will we be able to nourish our relationships. Only then will we truly be available and interruptible for the purposes of God.

What about you? Have you lost your joy and passion? Do you suffer from work dread? Are your relationships strained from stress? Do you wish you could check into a hospital just to sleep?

Understand that you are not alone. These symptoms are not a figment of your imagination. Instead you are suffering from a virulent new disease: the overload syndrome. Welcome to the new majority experience.

In this book we will examine the syndrome that is taking our margin away. Where does overload come from? What does it look like? What will it lead to? Most importantly, what can we do about it? With each overload, prescriptions will be offered that can counteract its effects, restoring needed time to rest and space to heal.

PART ONE

■ ■ ■ ■ ■ ■ ■ ■ ■

Defining
and
Understanding
Overload

CHAPTER 1

■ ■ ■ ■ ■ ■ ■

Overload and the Reality of Human Limits

In his famous story, "How Much Land Does a Man Need?,"[1] Tolstoy tells of the ambitious peasant Pakhom, who, after gaining ever greater plots of land, finally heard of a wonderful deal in a far-off country. He traveled to the land of the Bashkirs and negotiated with the village elder, who seemed a fool. The elder told Pakhom that he could have all the land he wanted for a thousand rubles a day.

Pakhom did not understand. "What kind of rate is that—a *day?*" he asked. "How many acres could that be?"

"We don't reckon your way. We sell by the day. However much you can walk around in one day will be yours."

When Pakhom expressed that a man can walk around much land in one day, the elder burst out laughing. "And all of it will be yours!" he replied. But there was one condition: If Pakhom didn't return to the starting point by sundown, the money would be forfeited.

Ecstatic, Pakhom spent a sleepless night. Rising at dawn, he went with the villagers to the top of a hill where the elder put down his hat. After placing his thousand rubles on top, Pakhom began walking, digging holes along the way to mark his land. The going was easy and he thought, "I'll do another three miles and then turn left. The land's so beautiful here, it would be a pity to miss any."

Pakhom hurried throughout the morning, going out of his way to add more land. But at noon when he looked back at the hill where he had begun, it was difficult to see the people. *Maybe I have gone too far,* he worried, and decided he must begin to make shorter sides. As the afternoon wore on, the heat was exhausting. By now his bare feet were cut and bruised, and his legs weakened. He wanted to rest, but it was out of the question.

Pakhom struggled on, walking faster, then running. He worried that he had been too greedy and his fear made him breathless. On he ran, his shirt soaked and his throat parched. His lungs were working like a blacksmith's bellows, his heart beat like a hammer. He was terrified. *All this strain will be the death of me.*

Although Pakhom feared death, he couldn't stop. *They'd call me an idiot,* he thought. When he was close enough to hear the Bashkirs cheering, he summoned his last ounce of strength and kept running. As he finally reached the hill, everything suddenly became dark—the sun had set. Pakhom groaned. He wanted to stop, but heard the Bashkirs still cheering him on. He realized that from where he was at the bottom of the hill, the sun had set—but not for those on top. Pakhom took a deep breath and rushed up the hill. Reaching the top, he saw the elder sitting by the hat, laughing his head off. Pakhom's legs gave way, and he fell forward grasping the cap.

"Oh, well done!" exclaimed the elder. "That's a lot of land you've earned yourself!"

Pakhom's worker ran up and tried to lift his master, but Pakhom was dead. The worker picked up Pakhom's spade, dug a grave, and buried him—six feet from head to heel, exactly the amount of land a man needed.

The Autopsy

In a modern setting Pakhom would have fit in nicely on Wall Street. Or Main Street. Perhaps he even stares at us each morning from our bathroom mirrors. By asking post-mortem questions about Pakhom, let's see if we can't catch a glimpse of what is wrong with our own lives.

Pakhom most likely died from a heart attack or a heat stroke brought on by overexertion. But on another level, did he die of running? Does this mean that running is bad for you? Of course not. Running is good for you. Unless, of course, it is *too much* running. *Too much* running can be bad. It can even be fatal.

Did Pakhom die of ambition? Does this mean that wanting land is unhealthy? No, unless it is *too much* land. That, too, apparently can kill.

It is not wrong to run, to have ambition, to want a farm, to expand the farm, to dig holes. Still, Pakhom died. Stone, cold dead. He died from overload.

Overload is that point when our limits are exceeded. Tolstoy's story is a powerful illustration of the reality of limits and the health implications of exceeding them. The Bashkirs knew that Pakhom's body had limits—but his greed did not.

In the same way, today many are harming themselves through the temptation to do more than their limits will allow. Walking, running, and ambition are not necessarily unhealthy. *Too much,* however, is universally unhealthy.

Overload is like that. The problem is not with *load.* The problem is with *over.*

Generally speaking, *loads* are a good thing. We would be hopelessly bored without them. As a matter of fact, even though this is an *anti-overload* book, I am a *pro-load* person. Load is not the enemy. Overload is.

UNIVERSAL LIMITS

Do you have a well-developed psychology of human limits? Perhaps even more importantly, do you have a well-developed theology of human limits? To clarify this issue, let's examine two questions:

1. *Do we have limits?*
2. *If we have limits, where did they come from?*

Do We Have Limits?

Do we? All of us? Of course we do. Every person has limits—no exceptions. We see limits everywhere we look. One could even say there is a law of limits, both in our human experience and in the physical universe.

Yet many people act under the illusion that there are no human limits. Many managers grow quickly impatient with such talk. Many employers continually insist that those under them do more and more with less and less. Many Type A's (a personality type that is driven and hypercompetitive, with carburetors stuck on high) live in chronic denial. Many Christians assume that God has, in fact, given them a special exemption.

It is true, of course, that many individuals have accomplished stunning feats. One person, for example, memorized the non-repeating number pi to thirty thousand digits. Some climb Mt. Everest without oxygen. Some run a marathon in Nepal at an average elevation of fourteen thousand feet. Dramatic stuff.

After reading of such accomplishments, we might be tempted to assume that humans have almost unlimited powers. But when we take such an assumption at face value and adopt it as a life motto, we can find ourselves in deep trouble—heart attacks, work dread, ruined relationships, exhaustion, depression, and burnout. Many are already there. And many more are dangerously close.

Recently I mentioned to a friend that humans will never run a one-minute mile. He paused briefly and then said, "Never say never."

Think about this. With whom do you agree? Do you agree with my friend and insist that someone might eventually run the mile in one minute, as unlikely as that seems? Or do you agree with my assertion that it is humanly impossible?

If you paused to consider the possibility, I am sympathetic to that pause. It is right to consider whether this assertion seems true or not before answering. But just the fact that we are willing to even consider the possibility of a one-minute mile in itself illustrates the fact that we have a problem truly accepting our limits.

Of course we all wish to be careful making such pronouncements as "the one-minute mile is humanly impossible." In the past, people have made predictions and then ended up looking foolish when later proved wrong. But I want to force you into a position here. If you refuse to make the statement that we will never be able to run a one-minute mile, then let's push further. How about thirty seconds? If you still hold out, then how about five seconds? Eventually, you will have to agree that we have limits.

The position I am taking is not always popular. We are so accustomed to pushing the limits—even exalting that push—that we often completely skip over the fact that we do, in fact, have limits. We all do. It is undeniable. Everything on earth has limits.

Again this is not a popular argument to make. Many of our leaders, thinkers, inventors, and motivators are teaching us to think big, to think of all the possibilities, to assault the impossible. And that's good. But we must be careful and we must be precise, for there is another side to this issue that often remains unexpressed. When we start to pretend that somehow we don't have limits, we get ourselves mired in painful consequences.

For many well-meaning Christians, my argument almost sounds like heresy. I recently saw a T-shirt that said "No limits," with three or four Bible verses backing up the slogan. But the Bible never says that we are unlimited. It says that God is unlimited. There is a difference. This brings us to our second question.

If We Have Limits, Where Did They Come From?
Are limits the result of the Fall or were they God's idea? In other words, did limits come into the world with sin and death or did God create them intentionally?

Limits were God's intention from the beginning. He decided early on that limits were not only good but necessary. It was His way of preempting any ambiguity about who is God and who is not. He is the Creator—the One without limits. We are the created—the ones with limits.

The fact is, we often get into all kinds of trouble by inflating our role in the drama of life. Perhaps this is one of the main reasons why God created limits. He knew that without limits, we would overreach, swell with pride, and become independent. We would get priorities all messed up, and life balance would be neglected. He would have been right. So to address that problem preemptively, He created limits.

We are not infinite. None of us has more than twenty-four hours in a day. We do not have an inexhaustible source of human energy. We cannot keep running on empty. Limits are real and, despite what some stoics might think, limits are not even an enemy. Overload is the enemy.

As the author of limits, God put them within us for our protection. We violate them at our peril. God is under no moral obligation to bail us out of our pain if we attempt to do more than He asks.

GOD THE CREATOR . . . OF LIMITS

For some, to say that we have limits seems to limit God. But saying that *we* have limits in no way suggests that *God* has limits. And to say that all the spiritual work in the kingdom must be done with human effort misses the point of God's power altogether. It is very freeing to realize that God has the resources to get the job done, and that rest is still a part of His will for us. Conversely, it is lack of faith—coupled with an inadequate view of God—to think that we have to work twenty-hour days to get everything done. Far from dishonoring God by acknowledging human limits, it dishonors Him to *deny* limits. It insults His creation wisdom.

I am not out to thwart our accomplishments or encourage us toward mediocrity. Mediocrity and I are not friends. Instead, I am only warning us not to trust our own strength but to give God full credit for the fact that He gets the work done. It is, after all, His world, His work, and His power. "But we have this treasure in jars of clay," explained the apostle Paul, "to show that the all-surpassing power is from God and not from us."[2]

NO EXCEPTIONS, NO EXEMPTIONS

Over the past decade I have given hundreds of presentations on margin, human limits, and overload. If I had a nickel for every time someone asked me about the role of personality variation on perceived overload, I could make a down payment on the solar system.

Personality, genetics, culture, values, expectations, ethnic background, family system, work ethic—all play a tremendous role in determining how the topic of overload applies to each individual life. Therefore, the issue of the variability of human personality must be an important aspect of the discussion whenever attempting to have a balanced view of overload on the individual level.

There are two generalizations we can make about this topic:
1. *Everyone is different.* These differences must be taken into account when we talk about the issue of human limits.
2. *Everyone is the same.* Limits exist, and the universality of that fact ultimately holds sway over all dissenting views.

Everyone Is Different

God created us extraordinarily diverse. We are all variations on a theme and the variations are endless. God invented chromosomes and genetics and decided to use the human genome to accomplish His creative human artistry.

Each nucleus of each cell has twenty-three pairs of chromosomes. If we were to combine all the chromosomal material from one cell together, we would have the human genome. Imprinted on our human genome is everything about our physical nature, as well as much about our personality and emotional makeup. In each cell, this human genome contains eighty thousand genes. They are all encoded on tightly coiled DNA and three billion base pairs per cell. This human code is unique to each person.

God did something quite remarkable along the lines of diversity, and it seems to me that we ought, at minimum, to acknowledge it. Instead of kicking against it, we should recognize this, accept it, even celebrate it.

Someone once said that foreign travel is when we pay a lot of money to go to a place where things are different and then complain because they aren't the same. In many ways, God made us different for a reason, yet we complain incessantly because others aren't the same as us. I have a feeling God was right to make us different from one another. Imagine how boring the world would be if everyone were a clone of me. *I* wouldn't even want to live there.

Everyone Is the Same

On the other hand, all of the billions of people on the earth are the same in one important dimension—we all have limits. No one is infinite. We all need to sleep, to eat, to exercise, and to rest. The extent to which we need to do these things varies tremendously. Yet we all hit our personal limits at some point. Despite our enormous diversity, we are all bound together by this similarity of limits.

For every limit there is a threshold. Somewhere a line can be drawn for every human being to represent such a threshold. True, we would have to draw this line in a different place for each person, but the fact remains—we can draw such a line *somewhere*. Even people who never thought they would reach their limits are hitting the wall under the fast-paced conditions of modernity. That threshold, which once seemed so distant and theoretical, is now a painful reality for us all.

Combining these two generalizations, we see that for each person we can draw a line that represents the threshold of his or her personal limits, but for each person that line will be drawn at a different place compared to others.

Exceptional People Maybe—but No Exceptions

What about those extraordinary people who seem to accomplish so very much and never get weary? People who only sleep two hours a night, or who create a hundred million dollar business in just five years, or who have ten children and a sixty-hour job as a corporate executive, yet get voted "parent of the year"?

Indeed such stories are breathtaking. But this does not mean that I should feel guilty if God has not given me those same abilities. We should not be in the business of telling God how He should arrange the personalities in His kingdom. It is, after all, His kingdom, and He has the right to do with it as He wants.

These exceptional people are interesting and their accomplishments laudable. But remember, even exceptional people have limits. Unfortunately if we follow many of them into the future, we often would find the same painful consequences of chronic limit violation the rest of us experience: physical illness, emotional burnout, relational strain.

THREE CASES

Let's examine three different circumstances to learn what they can tell us about how personalities and beliefs influence our discussion of overload.

Highly Productive People (HPP)

At one end of the spectrum are those in our midst obviously wired for a higher level of involvement, activity, and achievement than the rest of us. They get by on less sleep, always seem to have energy to spare, rise to the top of organizations, and in general, lead the charge into the future. For purposes of simplification, let's simply call them highly productive people (HPP)—those in the top ten percent of productivity. They have several specific things to teach us about overload—both positive and negative.

The highly productive person accomplishes a great deal. These extraordinary people accomplish more before 9 A.M. than the rest of us do all month. Much of our national success can be attributed to their efforts. They do much of the work, make most of the decisions, develop most of the new products, and create most of the wealth that the rest of us have grown to depend on.

The highly productive person has a remarkable work ethic. The work ethic practiced by HPPs is extraordinary. They have a special capacity for putting in long hours, staying focused, and still maintaining energy and passion. Persistent and persevering are often good descriptors.

The highly productive person often has great vision. Even in the midst of the smoke and fire of overload that disable the efforts of others, HPPs can see where they need to go and are determined to get there. They have the vision of an eagle and the jaws of a pit bull. Once they sink their teeth into a project they believe in, they are not about to let go.

The highly productive person often lacks good warning signals. All of us lack adequate warning signals for overload and do not realize that we are overloaded until we feel the pain. Unfortunately HPPs often find themselves at an even greater disadvantage. While others might be able to tell that something is wrong when they are at one hundred and ten percent, HPPs often don't realize they are seriously overloaded until they are at one hundred and forty percent. And by that time, there is nothing left to do but crash and burn.

The highly productive person sometimes sets up unrealistic standards for others. Because achievement comes so easily to HPPs, they will often set the bar high and then kill themselves trying to live up to it. That may be okay for them. But often they will require this same level of unrealistic commitment from others. Trying to motivate others is a good goal, but when we are trying to motivate others to join us in a high-energy lifestyle, we need to be sure that we are indeed speaking for God.

The highly productive person often doles out acceptance based on performance. We get paid for what we do and that is the way it should be. And if we don't do anything, we will never go anywhere. It is called justice. The performance-based approach to life contains in it a certain reality that is undeniable. However, HPPs often have an inflated sense that performance is *all* that matters.

When the world they control becomes structured in this way, those who do not have high energy and productivity tend to linger further behind. Or they will experience chronic overload trying to keep up with people who are wired more advantageously.

Performance deserves to be *one* criteria by which acceptance is handed out. But it should not be the only criteria — or even the main criteria. We must always be careful to value most what God values — things like love, compassion, service, justice, faithfulness, purity, prayer, obedience, kindness, and gentleness.

Highly Sensitive People (HSP)

On the other end of the spectrum from the high-energy, highly productive people are the highly sensitive people (HSP). (This is not to imply that they are unproductive, but just that their personality structure is very different from the HPP.) The highly sensitive person has been well described by psychologist Elaine N. Aron in her 1996 book by that title.[3] HSPs, we could perhaps say, are in the top ten percent of sensitivity (Aron uses the figure fifteen to twenty percent). They often find themselves chronically overwhelmed by excessive sensory input.

The highly sensitive person has antennae up for social discord or discomfort. They can feel the pain in the room. They can read the faces. Even with subtle indicators, they can tell when the social hierarchy is being unkind. They are also particularly susceptible to the insults and violence on television and in other media.

The highly sensitive person sometimes seems antisocial. Because they pay a price for social interaction, they don't venture out as much. They might be more socially isolated. It takes longer for them to heal. Their batteries are discharged by all of this continuous and chronic sensitivity vigilance. It does not mean that they are truly reclusive, but just that they are worn down by the requirement of excessive sensitivity.

The highly sensitive person is often creative. They live in a world in their heads. They are good company for themselves on long car trips, and they don't mind solitude. They dream a lot. They don't try to control others' lives, because they intuitively understand how complicated that process is.

The highly sensitive person is more susceptible to overload. They pay a higher emotional price for almost everything. It is like the world's loudspeaker is always on for them. They wear down more quickly. They must pay special heed to the words of this book. These interesting people make a special contribution to the world, but often at a greater emotional price than others. They give something that no one else can in quite the same way—sensitivity.

A Christian Exemption?

Finally, let's consider one other category—Christians. Are believers equipped with some kind of stress exemption? Do they ever burn out? These might sound like heretical questions. Nevertheless, the issue is important to consider. Because if we answer the question incorrectly—in either direction—there will be significant consequences.

Many people with great faith assume that God gives them a

special exemption to stress, overload, and burnout. It therefore comes as a great surprise when they, too, hit the wall.

How could this happen to me? I must not have had enough faith.

Disillusionment sets in. Then discouragement. We stop ministering. We have no permission to tell others of our pain. What to do? Sadly, we sometimes find ourselves trapped in a system that provides no comfort—only judgment.

Overload, just like influenza, is a nonsectarian pathogen. It strikes indiscriminately. Believers experience overload just like we experience the flu when it comes to town. We have the same limits and susceptibilities as everyone else.

As it turns out, salvation solves the lostness problem—of incalculable value. But it does little to solve the overload problem. This is not to say we don't have deep spiritual resources. But in some ways, we also have a heightened sensitivity to the pain and brokenness of the world around us. And often that hurts unbearably.

God had His reasons for not delivering us from this pain. It is best to trust His heart in the matter.

FAITH OR PRESUMPTION?

Sorting through the broad applications of the stress-limits-overload issue takes time. Unfortunately, our practicality and theology have not yet had the opportunity to catch up to the rapid changes all around us. We are still trying to figure out where to draw the line between faith and presumption. It is a very important line.

Beware of the presumption of overextending. What happens if we are out on a limb, doing one hundred and fifty percent of what we ought and then get into trouble? We cry out to God, "Help!"

But God replies, "When you come back to where you belong, then I will help you. Remember: *You* are the creature. *I* am God. Use My power, not your own."

Nevertheless, because this is such a difficult lesson for us to learn in our performance-driven, activity-oriented culture, we see people working eighteen-hour days for laudable causes, neglecting their relationships . . . only to have their spouses leave or their children become alienated.

We see others doing wonderful service for God and humankind but depriving their bodies of sleep, nutrition, exercise. Then comes the heart attack at age forty-eight.

We see delightful, well-meaning servants who overcommit and then wonder why they have no joy.

We see physicians who are so chronically overworked that they resent their patients for being ill.

And on it goes. And on . . . and on. . . .

Fatal Flaw

Ultimately the driven notion that we must relentlessly pursue activity every waking minute is fatally flawed—both practically and theologically. If we insist that we must be "all things to all people all the time all by ourselves"; that God requires no less than total, all-out, burnout effort; that it would insult Christ's sacrifice for us to rest; that there are too many opportunities for us to slow down— then we will find ourselves backed up against a logical juggernaut. If these arguments hold, then how could we defend ever ceasing our efforts?

For example, if after a productive, busy day you finally quit at midnight, I would go to your house and greet you on the front step. The conversation might go like this.

"Are you done for today?" I would ask.

"Yes. Finally. A long day—seventeen hours. But all important things. It was an exhausting day—but a good one."

"Why are you quitting now?" I would ask.

"Well, because it's midnight."

"So it is. Does that mean that all your work is done? Isn't there *something* that you could be doing? Isn't there some good that you could still pursue? Isn't there some need you could work on? Some studying . . . or perhaps letters of encouragement to write?"

"Give me a break!" you would say. "What do you expect?"

Exactly my point. Whenever we quit for the day, it is always arbitrary. The world is not yet perfect—but we ceased our efforts? There is still more to be done—and yet we are going to sleep? The fact is, whenever we quit we are abandoning the job unfinished.

Because *the job can never be finished.*

Life is always a process, and it is the *process* that God is concerned with more than *productivity.* He knows perfectibility is not possible and that all our labors are feeble against the brokenness of the world. When we overly emphasize *productivity* (a typically American thing to do), we often pervert the *process:* instead of faith, we substitute work; instead of depth, we substitute speed; instead of love, we substitute money; instead of prayer, we substitute busyness.

God does not give out monthly productivity sheets. All He asks is "Do you love Me?" Such love is not measured by units per hour (productivity), but rather by consistently loving the person standing in front of you at the moment (process). It does not have to do with the past nor the future, but the present. Right now. Are you bringing the kingdom of God to bear on whatever you are doing — right now?

Let's take the world of medical practice as an example. A productivity model would say that if I see thirty patients a day rather than twenty, I am a better doctor. Rewards will follow. Does this mean that seeing fifty patients is better than thirty? One hundred patients is better than fifty? Obviously, as *productivity* is pushed to extremes, *process* begins to suffer. I can tell you from experience that an overemphasis on medical productivity displaces caring, compassion, and service.

God does not have to depend on human exhaustion to get His work done. God is not so desperate for resources to accomplish His purposes that we have to abandon the raising of our children in order to accommodate Him. God is not so despairing of where to turn next that He has to ask us to go without sleep five nights in a row. Chronic overloading is not a spiritual prerequisite for authentic Christianity. Quite the contrary, overloading is often what we do when we forget who God is.

Our contemporary drivenness assumes that God never reaches down and says, "Enough, my child. Well done. Now go home and love your children. Encourage your spouse. Rest. Pray. Meditate. Sleep. Recharge your batteries. I'll have more for you to do tomorrow. And, by the way, don't worry. Remember who you are dealing with."

IT'S OKAY WITH GOD

Since God is the author and creator of my limits, then it is probably okay with Him that I have limits. He probably does not expect me to be infinite and is a little surprised when I try. It is okay with Him if I am not all things to all people all the time all by myself. As a matter of fact, it is probably *not* okay with Him if I assume otherwise.

You see, it is okay for me to have limits—God doesn't.

It is okay to get a good night's sleep—God doesn't sleep.

It is okay for me to rest—God doesn't need to.

It is probably even okay to be depressed—because God isn't.

We do not know a lot about what heaven looks like, but this much we know: God is not pacing the throne room anxious and depressed because of the condition of the world. He knows, He is not surprised, and He is sovereign.

It is okay if we have limits. He is able.

CHAPTER 2

■ ■ ■ ■ ■ ■ ■

Blame Progress

During medical school, Linda and I traveled to India for a summer of hospital volunteering. Flying into Bombay, we knew it was monsoon season and expected to get wet. Our arrival at the airport was a soaking one. After collecting our bags, we peered past the teeming hoards to see that outside it was still raining hard. Actually, the density of rainfall looked more like someone had lifted the ocean a mile above Bombay and then dumped it on top of the airport.

Later, we learned that ours was the only flight to land that day. Roads were flooded and the traffic was paralyzed. A rare taxi took us as far as he could into town, charging exorbitant rates. We paid the inflated fare and stepped out of the cab into six inches of water mixed with—whatever. Taking off my shoes and socks, I lifted the suitcases to my shoulders. We surely made some sight—foreigners without a clue, sloshing down unknown Bombay streets with floating garbage bumping into our ankles.

So, this is summer in India! we thought. We had heard of monsoons and found it all quite adventurous.

The next morning's headlines, however, stunned us: "Eighteen inches in twenty-four hours—largest rainfall in eighty-five years!" It wasn't just a monsoon we had experienced the day before—it was an *unprecedented* monsoon. It wasn't just a rain, it was an *historic* rain. And even though we stood in the middle of it, we had no idea that history was being made at our ankles.

HISTORICALLY UNPRECEDENTED

Such failure to recognize the historic dimensions of current events is not unusual. Even when we experience the historic as it happens, most of us remain unaware of its significance. Even when we are being personally victimized by unprecedented events, still we do not understand. We assume today is "every day" when in fact it is "like no other day."

Let us now return to our discussion of overload and limits. Why, *at this point in history*, are we discussing limits? Is there something afoot that causes this discussion to be particularly timely and relevant? Indeed. Something is happening on our generational shift, and it is historically unprecedented. The universe has seizured, destabilizing everything at the same time. Yet we just keep eating and sleeping, buying and selling—all the time failing to realize that *this* deluge is different. These current developments are historically, experientially, mathematically, and spiritually unprecedented on a scale that staggers our thinking. Unfortunately, our day-to-day routine provides no frame of reference with which to assess such occurrences.

Perhaps an apt comparison would be a raft floating down a river. The raft is our life, its four sides defining the limits of our existence. Every morning we awaken to—the same raft. Of course, we are aware that there is water surrounding the raft, but every morning it also seems about the same. Our perceptions fail us here. For even though the raft stays the same, the river does not. First, the river picks up speed. Almost imperceptibility at first. Then the river gets deeper—but that is also unknown to us.

Then the river gets wider. Slowly at first, so we are not aware of day-to-day changes. Finally, the river gets rougher. The waves are higher than we remember them. The shoreline is barely perceptible and goes by in a blur. We begin to grow uneasy. Still, all we see is the raft.

Similarly, our lives float in a culture. Our lives continue to be the same twenty-four hours a day — work eight hours, sleep seven hours, eat three times. All the while, the cultural flow becomes faster, rougher, and blurred. Taking refuge in the boundaries of our raft, we pretend that because the dimensions of our raft have not changed, nothing else has changed either. There is, after all, "nothing new under the sun."

Until we plummet over the falls.

SUDDENNESS

Not only are these changes *unprecedented* in a way hard to imagine, but they are also *sudden*. Suddenness, perhaps, like the million-dollar house in southern California that burned to the ground in ten minutes. In the same way, historically speaking, contemporary overloading happened in the blink of an eye.

Before our current overload crisis I doubt most of us gave much thought to the issue of limits. Perhaps we assumed limits would arrive in a slow, discernible manner. We thought we would see the thresholds coming and could adapt to these interesting changes in a paced way. Unfortunately that has not been the case. The limits came at us too many, too fast. People hit the wall and then scratch their heads in confusion and disbelief.

Let me give you two mathematical illustrations to help you gauge what I am referring to.

First, a quiz about exponential change.

To support dairy farmers in our home state of Wisconsin, the loyal thing is to eat ice cream. If I were to double my ice cream consumption every year — one teaspoon of ice cream at age one, two teaspoons at age two, four teaspoons at age three, and so on — how much would I be eating at age fifty? Answer: Fifty-two tons per second.

Second, a quiz about big numbers.

If at a rate of one digit per second, you were to count to a million, how long would it take? Answer: Ten days. Now, counting at the same rate, skip a billion and count to a trillion. How long would it take? Answer: Thirty-two thousand years.

Our intuition is not capable of approximating the answers to these two questions. In the first instance, we do not know how to estimate exponential change—even though exponential change is happening all around us. (For a more complete discussion of this important phenomenon, see *Margin* Part One and Appendix for graphs.)[1] In the second instance, we do not understand big numbers and have no frame of reference by which to assess them. Our national debt, for example, is five trillion dollars—and there is not a person alive who knows what five trillion dollars means.

In many ways, these two illustrations describe both our experience and our problem. Fifty-two tons per second and thirty-two thousand years speak to the radical sudden dimension of change we are experiencing. So much has changed so fast that we lag significantly behind the curve in understanding both its dimensions and its practical implications.

MORE AND MORE, FASTER AND FASTER

If life is changing this dramatically, why is it happening? And why is it happening *now?* Many forces contribute to the overload of our age, but dominant among them—surprisingly—is progress.

Progress has been wonderful in many regards. It has given us thousands of advantages over earlier eras: education and communication, medical technologies and antibiotics, convenience and comfort—advancements almost beyond imagination. But, like everything else in a flawed world, progress has a downside. And that downside has much to do with overload.

Progress works by *differentiating our environment*. For example, if we cut down a tree, bring it into the garage, and instruct progress to differentiate the log, it would make tables, chairs, baseball bats, fruit bowls, and toothpicks—that is, many varied wood products. Understanding this *differentiation* is the key to understanding *progress*. And understanding *progress* is the key to understanding *overload*.

The functional result of such differentiation is that progress always gives us *more and more of everything faster and faster.* Getting more and more of everything is wonderful—as long as that is what we need. When saturated, however, getting more and more of everything faster and faster becomes a problem.

Most of us don't need *more.* And we certainly don't need it *faster.* Instead of being our friends, *more* and *faster* have now become our twin enemies. Instead of bringing benefit, more and faster often bring us pain—the pain of overload.

If thirsty, it would be unsatisfying to drink water through an eye dropper. That's too little water. We want more and we want it faster. But it would be even more unsatisfying to drink from a fire hose. That's too much, coming too fast! We don't need our sinuses irrigated—we just want a drink of water.

Progress is acting like a fire hose. And our sinuses have never been cleaner.

Pushy Progress

"Progress," someone once said, "is where we work very hard to make things as good as they used to be." Observed another critic, "Progress is the future you envisioned yesterday but didn't like when you woke up today."

Such sentiments have become commonplace at the turning of the millennium. But why do we express this ambivalence? A major reason for our cynicism: overload. People have been pushed to their limits—and beyond. Often, it was progress that did the pushing.

There are only so many details that can be comfortably managed in anybody's life. Once this number has been exceeded, one of two things happens: disorganization or frustration. Yet progress gives us more and more details every year—often at exponential rates. We have to deal with more "things per person" than ever before in the history of humankind. As a result, overload is not only real, it is pathogenic.

Every year we have more products, more information, more technology, more activities, more choices, more change, more traffic, more commitments, more work. In short, more of everything. Faster.

This ubiquitous overloading is a natural function of progress. It is automatic. If we sit meekly and do nothing about it, next year at this time, we will be even more overloaded than we are right now.

ONE-WAY STREET

Progress, in many ways, can't help itself. It has only been taught to go in one direction: differentiation. This is precisely what we have asked and expected of progress. Who in their right mind would expect progress to give us *less and less, slower and slower?* We have, therefore, built our way of life—and our economy—around this differentiation.

As a result, if we were to slow progress, our economy would fall apart. To date, that lacks bipartisan support. Yet, on the other hand, if we do not slow the tidal wave of overloading at the hands of progress, we will fall apart. That, too, lacks bipartisan support.

In such a tug of war between progress and the economy on the one hand, and the problem of overloading on the other, progress and the economy will win. Hands down. The economy *always* wins. Therefore, progress is not going to slow down. We can count on *more and more* from here on out.

It is time for an axiom: *Progress automatically leads to increasing overload, marginlessness, speed, change, stress, and complexity.*

- ■ Overload: Most of us now live beyond the threshold of our limits, and progress is not going to reverse that trend.
- ■ Marginlessness: Margin is the space between our load and our limits. Progress has taken this therapeutic space away.
- ■ Speed: Every year, the speed of the treadmill goes faster. Buckle your seat belt.
- ■ Change: Future Shock arrived some time ago, and there is no deceleration in sight.
- ■ Stress: Stress is our adaptation to change. As change increases, so does stress.
- ■ Complexity: The flow of progress is always in the direction of increasing complexity.

Because progress only knows how to travel in one direction, these six saboteurs of progress are not self-correcting. Mark them well— they are after you.

THE ROLE OF TECHNOLOGY

If progress is the train driving us to the land of overload, technology is the engine. They work hand in hand. Just as they have been partners in bringing us benefit, so they have partnered together in the crime of overload. Did you realize, for example, that the average American has to learn how to operate twenty thousand pieces of technology? What could better illustrate contemporary overload than that single statistic?

As we begin to examine specific overloads in Part Two it will become apparent how technology plays an integral role in each— and how *resisting* technology plays an equally important role in the suggested prescriptions. Accessibility overload, for example, is only possible because accessing technologies are now so mobile and miniaturized we have no excuse left for not being on-call for the universe. Media overload has exploded precisely because technology has given us a telecommunications revolution unprecedented in human history. There is now even a television set that can be worn on the head. (And you thought Walkmans were annoying.) Activity overload is only possible because the technologies of transportation and communication both stimulate and facilitate it.

If, as an illustration, you picture *progress* as the entire world, imagine *technology* as the Pacific Ocean, and each specific *overload* as an island within that ocean. Because progress runs our economy, and because technology propels the engine for so much of progress, don't look for either to slow anytime soon. Yet it is easier, on an individual level, to resist technology than it is to stand in the way of progress. Simplicity is still an option. We can't leave the earth. But we can always move away from the Pacific.

WARNING SIGNS

As progress and technology careen out of control downhill, increasing overload, marginlessness, speed, change, stress, and complexity will inevitably follow. Even the highest levels of privilege and power are not exempt. Recently, for example, I had the honor of speaking with some members of Congress about these concepts. In response to a question from one congressman about what symptoms accompany stress and overload, I listed about twenty: *psychological symptoms* such as anxiety, depression, confusion, negative thinking; *physical symptoms* such as headaches, unexplained fatigue, indigestion, increased infections; *behavioral symptoms* such as irritability, withdrawal, driving too fast. As I finished, another asked: "What does it mean if you have *all* of those symptoms?"

What are the warning signs that overload is upon us? How do we know when we are approaching the threshold line of our limits? To illustrate, let's look at three scenarios: eighty percent full (margined), one hundred percent full (maximized), and one hundred and twenty percent full (overloaded).

Eighty Percent Full

On the unsaturated side of our limits, we can be open and expansive. We can say yes to new opportunities and activities with enthusiasm because there is space to put them.

Our boss asks: "Can you work overtime this weekend?" *I'd be glad to! I enjoy my work, I've got the time, and besides, who couldn't use a little extra money?*

Our church asks: "Can you teach Sunday school?" *Sure. It's great fun to be around kids and a privilege to teach them.*

Our spouse asks: "Can we take the neighbors out to dinner and a movie?" *That would be great. We have wanted to get together with them for months now.*

Living on the unsaturated side of our limits allows space for involvement without the complicating burden of unnecessary self-protection.

One Hundred Percent Full

As we straddle the line that represents the threshold of our limits, decisions become much harder. A strange ambivalence arises about any new decision.

Our boss comes to us and says: "Can you work overtime this weekend?" *I'm not sure . . . let me think about it . . . I'll have to get back to you . . . Oh, I guess I can.*

Our church asks: "Could you teach Sunday school?" *You know, that is something I have always wanted to do. But I'm kind of busy right now. I had better think it over and let you know next week.*

Our spouse asks: "Can we take the neighbors out to dinner and a movie?" *I don't think so, honey. Not this week anyway. Let's think about it for next week.*

This new ambivalence is uncomfortable, and we can't really explain it. We have never felt this way before, and wonder why it is so hard to make decisions about things we have always felt positively about in the past.

One Hundred and Twenty Percent Full

As we cross into overload, we find the land of saturation downright painful.

Our boss comes to us and says: "Can you work overtime this weekend?" *NO. As a matter of fact, I QUIT! I'm tired of people dumping all their problems on me.*

Our church asks: "Could you teach Sunday school?" *Are you kidding? I hate kids!!!*

Our spouse asks: "Can we take the neighbors out to dinner and a movie?" *I've got a better idea. Let's just pull down the shades and pretend we're not home.*

Once our lives are saturated, the rules totally change. We can't factor anything more into our lives until we take something equally time- or energy-consuming away. As elementary as this principle sounds, it nevertheless escapes most of us most of the time.

RECOGNIZING AND ACCEPTING OUR LIMITS

When we are overloaded, how can we tell? We are not very adept at knowing where our limits are, and most of us have never seriously thought about them—certainly not in any objective or scientific terms. Unfortunately, God did not equip us with reliable warning signals. There are no indicator lights that blink at ninety-five percent; no alarms that blare at one hundred percent. Often the first sign we have is pain.

When overloaded, joy has a tendency to disappear. We might develop a variety of physical symptoms. We become self-protective and begin resenting people for needing our help. Irritability, often directed at those we love the most, further damages our attitude.

Overload reminds us of two important truths:

- We are only human. It is best not to forget it.
- God, the author of our limits, will use these same limits freely to remind us that we have need of Him.

Prescriptions Against the Pain

Part One of this book is important because diagnostic accuracy matters. As someone once observed: "Problem resolution always begins with correct problem identification." We will not solve our problems until we correctly understand them.

But now that we have diagnosed *overload* as the new universal constant, what can we do about it? Let's shine a light down each corridor of our lives, searching for prescriptions against the pain of each specific overload we encounter.

PART TWO

■■■■■■■■

Relieving Contemporary Overloads

CHAPTER 3

■ ■ ■ ■ ■ ■ ■

Accessibility

■ I am dying of easy accessibility. If Alexander Graham Bell walked into my office, I'd punch him in the nose. If he called, you can be sure I'd put him on hold.
—JAMES M. CERLETTY, M.D.

■ The good news is, you're always connected to the office. The bad news is, you're always connected to the office.
—THE WALL STREET JOURNAL, FULL PAGE AD

■ Yuppie ear—A NEW SYNDROME WHERE PEOPLE ANSWER THEIR CELL PHONES IN THE MIDDLE OF THE NIGHT AND INADVERTENTLY STICK THE ANTENNA INTO THEIR EAR.

■ Beepilepsy—NEW NAME GIVEN TO THE MOMENTARY SEIZURE OF PANIC SUFFERED WHEN ONE'S PAGER GOES OFF.

The future arrived yesterday, when the Starship Enterprise landed in our backyard. Slick gadgets are strapped to every belt, plugged into every socket, and stuck in every ear. Overhead, still more gadgets swim in the heavenlies.

As telecommunications rapidly reshape the globe, we sit at the beginning of a universal connectivity unprecedented in human history. Cell phones and pagers, videophones and video-conferencing, telecommuting and fax machines, Internet and E-mail, satellites and the information superhighway. Images of futuristic excitement, to be sure.

But what will be the result of this incredible flurry of seemingly unstoppable activity—good or bad? Like most modern things, it will be both. At exactly the same time. The wheat and tares are growing side by side. On the "bad" side, the aspect of this development that disturbs me most is accessibility overload—the absence of hiding places. Privacy is going, going, gone. Natural solitude has disappeared.

INESCAPABILITY

A major unintended consequence of the flood of accessing technologies is that soon there will be no natural excuse for being unavailable. In the midst of our enthusiasm for the telecommunications revolution, we have not sufficiently discerned the horrifying psychic cost of what columnist William Safire has called *unrestrained reachability.* Don't get me wrong. I like people. Some of my best friends are people. But I also like to escape from time to time.

"Where were you all day? I tried to call you five times!" your boss or clients or in-laws or bridge partner will say. And because virtually everyone will carry tiny cell phones/pagers, you will have no excuse.

"I turned off my pager phone."

"You what?!!!"

What will this be like for exhausted pastors on vacation, maybe five states away, when a parishioner goes to the hospital? Do we disturb pastors for such occurrences? Most of us wouldn't. But some will—you can bet on it.

What if parishioners die? Do we interrupt pastors' much-needed vacations by requesting they return for the funeral? I spoke of this scenario recently at a Toronto pastors' retreat. Two of the pastors had agonized with this exact situation in the previous year. One returned home to do the funeral; the other didn't. The first disappointed his family and lost an important vacation. The second disappointed his church family and lost an important ministry opportunity. Both were victimized by progress and accessibility overload.

What about our employers? It goes without saying that most bosses are more invested in the job than the people they supervise. This often makes for a natural asymmetry between their expectations and those of the employees.

"Where were you yesterday?" the boss might ask. "I was trying to reach you all day!" Never mind that it was Saturday and we were camping with the children. Or that it was Christmas Day and we were halfway to Grandma's house.

The recent *Wall Street Journal* ad quoted at the beginning of this chapter flaunts this new and discomforting development. Both the good and the bad news is the same—we are always connected to the office. The advertisement, hawking a particular computer notebook, continues, "Being out of the office no longer means being out of touch. Connectivity has never been easier. Just think, your people will finally be able to stay connected around the clock. They'll just love that, won't they?"[1]

Lucent Technologies placed their own version of the same message, again in a full-page ad in the *Journal*: "A Formal Apology. Since inventing cellular and after introducing digital wireless, wireless office systems and cordless phones, it seems that anyone can get ahold of you no matter where you are. Sorry. Sincerely, Lucent Technologies."[2]

Physicians, who have been on-call since Adam broke his ankle chasing Eve, now find that requirement stretched to the insane extreme. "Telephones in our homes and offices, cordless phones in our backyards and cars, beepers, fax machines, and E-mail," complains Milwaukee physician James Cerletty. "It's enough to give you a stroke. . . . Albert Einstein said that the reason we are here on earth is for each other, but I don't think he envisioned how technology would erode our privacy. . . . What we have is an overload, a plethora, a supersaturation of communication. I'm dying of easy accessibility."[3]

PHONES

I don't recall always hating the telephone. But no ambiguity about that feeling exists today. How can one ever escape something as prevalent as mosquitoes and as audibly irritating as a chain saw?

"The telephone is one of those miracles one can discuss in terms either sacred or profane," explains Lance Morrow. "No one has yet devised a pleasant way for a telephone to come to life. The ring is a sudden intrusion, a drill in the ear. . . . The satanic bleats from some new phones are the equivalent of sound lasers.

"But the ring cannot be subtle. Its mission is disruption. . . . The telephone call is a breaking-and-entering that we invite by having telephones in the first place. Someone unbidden barges in and for an instant or an hour usurps the ears and upsets the mind's prior arrangements."[4]

Call Waiting
Call waiting, representing a "last-come, first-served" ethic, is like trying to choke out noxious weeds by planting thistles. But we don't like busy signals either. In a lifetime, the average American spends two years trying to call people who aren't in or whose line is busy. (Some of us, it seems, spend that much time annually.) So this is our choice: to be irritated by the busy signal or to be irritated by call waiting.

Answering Machines/Voice Mail
Answering machines are one of those things that we wish everyone else had but are sometimes glad we do not. My residential phone has never been graced with such a device. It is not that I wish to inconvenience those trying to contact us. But even less do I wish to return home at 11:00 P.M. and find out there are now five people I have to call. The answering machine slickly transforms *someone else's desire* to contact me into *my need* to return the call.

Junk Phone Calls
Unsolicited sales calls are yet another invasion of both privacy and sanity. Autodialing machines exist which can dial one hundred calls per hour in sequence, regardless of whether the phone is listed or not. My wife, Linda, recently received her fifth call asking us to become the proud owners of a GM Credit Card. Like the rest, it was refused. The notable thing about this call is that it arrived at 1:00 P.M. on a Sunday afternoon, just as we sat down to dinner. Monday through Saturday dinner—by now we are used to that. But Sunday dinner?

Menu-Driven Answering Systems
No discussion of modern telephone frustrations would be complete without mentioning automated menu-driven answering devices. Some have as many as ten options. I once tried calling America Online every day for thirty days to solve an on-line problem. Calling every hour of the day, including the middle of the night, the closest I ever came to reaching a living human being was thirty minutes ("If you wish to talk with our service department, the next

available representative will be with you in . . . (pause) . . . thirty minutes"). Finally, after a month, I contacted a young relative in Illinois who solved the problem in five minutes.

CELL PHONES

More than fifty million Americans own cell phones, with a new one being sold or given away every three seconds. The best thing to remember about such time-saving technologies is that they usually don't. The people with the most "time-saving technologies" are the same people with the highest blood pressure and fastest pulse.

A friend from Vail told us of her attempt to take twelve members of the exclusive Young Presidents Club hiking in the Colorado Rockies. At the first break, while overlooking a beautiful vista, seven of the twelve pulled out cell phones and called their offices. In Alaska, an avid salmon fisherman took three brokers out on the Russian River at 3:00 A.M. Before they even caught anything, the brokers were on their cell phones working the world markets.

One local telephone company advertises: "You need a cellular phone. It can save your life!" True. But knowing this, people are now taking risks they should not be taking and bringing along a cell phone to bail them out. Increasingly, mountain rescues are required for hikers and climbers who find it easier to pack their Motorola rather than all that safety equipment.

E-MAIL

In 1996, for the first time, the volume of E-mail sent exceeded the total amount of surface mail delivered. E-mail is fast and cheap. In many ways, it is a guy's stationery. To write a letter, first we have to find paper, pen, envelope, stamp, and address. And then we have to find the time. E-mail is much simpler.

As much as I dislike the phone, I like E-mail. It does not disturb me until I wish it to. I can answer it at my leisure and convenience. Sometimes (rarely) I do not answer it at all. But I recently heard of a man from California who was on vacation for a week.

When he returned, he had more than a thousand E-mail messages waiting for him. Just around the corner, this is the world waiting for us all.

Americans living abroad love E-mail. Except when they hate it. "Sometimes I feel that all I do is answer the mail," complains Dan, a missionary from Mexico. "When I travel for a few days, it's not uncommon to come back and get as many as one hundred messages that have to be read and answered." Susan, stationed in Mozambique, figures E-mail costs her about three dollars a page to receive. "That really adds up," she says, "especially for messages that aren't critical.

"One thing that bugs me is the short turnaround time churches expect," says another missionary. "I once received a three-page questionnaire to fill out with the request that I send it back within twenty-four hours for their missions conference. I received the E-mail at 5:15 P.M. Friday, and they wanted the information to compile on Saturday afternoon so they could use it on Sunday morning."[5] This is NOT to say that we should stop E-mailing our friends abroad—mostly this new technology has been a stunning success. But as with everything else, we should be both discerning and sensitive.

PAGERS

A few years back, my pager died from old age. Before I could celebrate, one of the graduating residents gleefully threw me his instrument. The pager number? 666. My first inclination was to throw it like a hand grenade. Then I thought it was perhaps a demonstration of God's sense of humor.

Do you worship in a church with physicians? If so, you undoubtedly have experienced the sound of a pager going off during the pastoral prayer. Beepers in church, in the movie theater, in weddings, in funerals—I have heard it all. Pager signals are one of the most dreadful noises ever invented to shake the brain loose from its tentative moorings. The beepilepsy startle is an involuntary reaction to which I have never accommodated.

Thankfully, many beepers today use the quiet vibrating mode.

This helps not only the sanity of the "beepee," but the rest of the world as well.

"I remember the days when there were signs outside our medical institutions that said: *Hospital Zone—Quiet Please,*" reminisces Dr. Cerletty. "Nowadays . . . beepers, monitors, and other noises make hospitals sound like a warmup act for a heavy metal rock band. Beepers burst onto the medical scene almost twenty years ago. The early models let out a sound so shrill that any dog within a two-mile radius began howling like a fifty-year-old with renal colic. Once doctors learned that calls could just as easily be from a used car salesman as a sick patient, beepers began to be 'inadvertently' misplaced or lost."[6]

HACKING, SPYING, STALKING, AND THE EVAPORATION OF PRIVACY

Telecommunication technologies have contributed to a deprivation of privacy unprecedented in human history. To date, much of this concern is more theoretical than actual. But the infrastructure exists, and the erosion of privacy has turned from a intermittent drip to a steady flow.

Joshua Quittner is the fully-wired news director of Time, Inc.'s information mega-mall. Recently, he was victimized by a prankster who rerouted the Quittner's home telephone to an out-of-state answering machine. Callers trying to reach them heard a voice identify himself as Mr. Quittner, who then said some extremely rude things. Next, the voice requested people to leave messages. This went on for several days until finally the ruse was suspected and phone service restored.

"It seemed funny at first. But the interloper continued to hit us again and again for the next six months. The phone company seemed powerless. Its security folks moved us to one unlisted number after another, half a dozen times. They put special PIN codes in place. They put traces on the line. But the troublemaker kept breaking through. . . .

"I remember feeling violated at the time. . . . Someone was invading my private space and there was nothing I or the authorities could do . . . it struck me that our privacy—mine and yours—has already disappeared."[7]

Let me say that I am not paranoid. Then let me point out that both you and I are being watched—either actually or potentially—every time we buy prescription drugs with company insurance, browse the Web, use a cellular phone, use credit cards, take out life insurance, register to vote, give our social security number, use an ATM, make a phone call, get checked out with a supermarket scanner, enter sweepstakes, use electronic tollway passes, send E-mail at work, or walk before a surveillance camera (which the average New Yorker does twenty times a day).[8]

Beginning with only your name and address, within a few hours any talented computer sleuth can find out what you do for a living, the names and ages of your spouse and children, what kind of car you drive, the value of your house and how much tax you pay on it, plus a detailed map of how to get to your home.

PRESCRIPTIONS FOR RESTORING PRIVACY TO OVER-ACCESSED LIVES

What can be done to counteract the accessibility overload syndrome's ill effects? How can we reestablish the needed privacy and solitude that permits a later reengagement with our needy world? Many steps can be taken—some to begin the process of restoration, others to guard against future erosion of important privacy needs.

Rx 1 *Be Discerning*
In a fallen world, all new technologies will have both positive and negative consequences. Our responsibility is to understand clearly this dynamic and then make day-to-day decisions regarding which consequence dominates.

It is not enough to look only at how much the technological trend is helping. We must, more importantly, also understand how much it is hurting. No amount of trendiness, pizzazz, or glitz should sway us. Nor should cultural or commercial pressure. Just because something is "good for business" is not sufficient reason to let it damage the spirit.

Rx 2 *Set Boundaries*

Caving in to demands that are emotionally overwhelming, relationally unhealthy, physically exhausting, and spiritually inauthentic is not the way to create the space and rest we all need. This dilemma is best solved by understanding and establishing boundaries.

The concept of boundaries suggests that it is acceptable and even desirable to erect and defend a perimeter around the private spaces of our lives. People have the right, for example, to establish the atmosphere in their own homes, regardless of the world's opinion on that issue.

In our family we have erected a sometimes loose boundary to protect the dinner hour: we do not answer the telephone during that time. Similarly, when the boys were young, we would not allow the telephone to disturb our evening routines of reading to them, praying with them, and tucking them in bed. No matter how important the phone call was, it could wait. As radical as this might sound, it is really simple common sense that has eluded us far too long.

Occasionally, when I am home alone and in a particularly drained state, I might not even answer the doorbell. After extensive speaking trips, I need to lie fallow, to do nothing, to recharge my batteries. It is not my desire to be rude or insensitive. But sometimes, I simply must rest.

Rx 3 *Control Interruptions*

The average middle manager in America, according to one study, is interrupted seventy-four times every day. Interruptions are a part of modern life, but with effort, they can be modified. Relocate to a quieter room. Go to the library to work. Work late at night or early in the morning. Have other people take messages for you and return them in a batched fashion. Control the telephone. Turn off the beeper. Employ technologies that block interruptions rather than cause them.

If interruptions were allowed during writing projects, I would give up in despair. An isolated setting away from home works best for me. Or when home, I routinely write through the night and then sleep after the sun comes up.

Rx 4 *Tame the Telephone*

Consider turning off or unplugging the telephone at selected times.

Consider getting an answering machine and letting it take calls when you are busy with more important things.

Consider using caller ID.

If you have call waiting, consider selectively turning it off before placing calls. Just press *70 and then enter the number you are calling. Call waiting automatically turns back on after each call.

For the more radically minded, consider getting an unlisted number. Forty percent of Californians have unlisted numbers, surely an accommodation to accessibility overload.

Even though our family has not gone to these lengths (except for turning off the phones, which we do often), I will not criticize those who choose these measures. Increasingly, in the face of advancing "unrestrained reachability," we will all develop an affinity for such protections.

Rx 5 *Deactivate the Answering Machine*

Just because we have an answering machine does not mean we have to leave it on all the time. If we find it overwhelming to come home to full voice mail, just turn it off. If the call is important, the person will call back.

Our family has never used an answering machine on our residential line. A second line to my study, however, has such a device. This second line exists primarily for the computer modem and sending faxes. However, not uncommonly I will give out this number so others can use the answering machine and not get caught playing "telephone tag."

Another suggestion—try this for your recorded message: "Please wait for the beep and hang up."

Rx 6 *Disconnect*

Consider selecting a personal or family "disconnect time"—a set time each day or a set evening each week. During disconnect time, shut out the external world. Announce to your friends, your relatives, your neighbors, your church, your work: "Every evening from 5:30 to 7:00, we are disconnecting. Don't try to reach us then because you won't be able to."

Rx 7 *Refuse Telephone Solicitation*
Set a consistent policy never to respond to telephone solicitations. Once you buy something from telemarketers, you're put on a "chump list" that's sold to other marketers. My advice—never buy.

Many pitches are for commercial products or services; other appeals are for charity. *When the call is for products or services,* politely refuse at the first instant without being rude. Then hang up. *When the call is for charity,* respond, "I'm sorry, but it is my policy to never respond to telephone solicitations. However, if you wish to send me materials in the mail, I will consider whether I should give to your cause."

Rx 8 *Remove Your Name*
Consider removing your name from many telemarketing and direct-mail lists. Write to:

(Telemarketing)	(Direct-mail list)
Direct Marketing Association	Direct Marketing Association
Telephone Preference Service	Mail Preference Service
P. O. Box 9014	P. O. Box 9008
Farmingdale, NY 11735	Farmingdale, NY 11735

To have your name and E-mail address removed from all electronic commercial mailing lists controlled by Cyber Promotions, send an E-mail with the words "Remove all" in the subject or message field to: remove@cyberpromo.com.

Rx 9 *Cell Phone—Take It or Leave It?*
I do not own a cell phone. After twenty years of being on call in medicine, I can't figure out why I should pay inflated rates to stay connected when I so desperately desire the opposite.

This, however, is not a sentiment shared by all doctors—nor should it be. A young female resident physician rose to the defense: "But I got a cell phone for Mother's Day and it's been great. Now, when I'm on call, I can take my baby for a stroller ride, or I can do an errand at the store." Exactly. If it serves your purposes and you are firmly in control, then use it. But if it is complicating and tyrannizing your already overloaded life, reject it.

In terms of safety—especially if you have young drivers—you may want to invest in a "pay-as-you-use" cell phone for emergency use only.

Personally, I'll buy one just after the Cubs win the World Series.

Rx 10 *Buy a Phoneless Cord*

Put a phoneless cord on your Christmas list. It could be the best gift you receive all year.

Rx 11 *Fix Your Cookie*

If computer security has you worried, rig your cookie. Your cookie is the little bits of code that identify you to cookie-catching websites. In other words, it is a software device dumped into your hard drive while you are visiting a website. The cookie continues to monitor your on-line activity even after you leave that site. It then feeds back information about your browsing habits the next time you reconnect to the parent website. Use your computer's Windows 95 "Find" command to get any file with the word "cookie" in its name. Look at it using a word-processing program to find out who is stashing cookies in your browser. To disable your cookie, go to website www.luckman.com and get a free "anonymous cookie," a program that disables cookies.[9]

Rx 12 *Retreat to a Motel*

Increasingly, overloaded people are checking into local motels just to escape. If you can afford it, this is a periodic option that the entire family might enjoy. Use an indoor pool during winter. Order a pizza, cuddle on the bed, and watch a family movie. Thirty years from now, it might remain as one of your children's most vivid memories.

In a variation on this theme, our church board sends our pastor out of town once a quarter for three days and two nights. He can tell no one where he is going; he has no agenda from the board; he goes alone or takes his wife; and he is to have no pulpit duties the following week. Our board does this because we appreciate our pastor. We want him to last. We feel that our church will have a healthier, more invested pastor for a longer period of time.

Rx 13 *Buy a Cabin*

Yes, this might decimate one's financial margin. But, on the other hand, it might also prevent a heart attack. Our family has never owned a second home, but several friends have purchased such "heart attack insurance." What might sound like a rationalization is really a sound emotional investment.

Buying a remote retreat with joint ownership might also present interesting possibilities for a church to build community. Inviting people to get away together for a weekend not only allows for needed escape but also accomplishes more relationship building in two days than might otherwise happen in ten years.

Rx 14 *Seek Solitude*

As accessibility overload arrives through the front door, *natural solitude* departs out the back. Fortunately, for the determined, *intentional solitude* is still attainable.

Use solitude for rest. Solitude is also of value in long-term creative projects. "To think and create," explains Janna Malamud Smith in her book *Private Matters,* "people often need solitude because its privacy allows not only mental continuity, quiet, and relief from feeling noticed, but latitude to experiment with half-formed ideas and ridiculous solutions."[10]

Use solitude to build a deeper relationship with God and self. If we do not make friends with God and self—if we do not cultivate an inner life—our aging will be fraught with loneliness. "It is solitude and solitude alone," observes theologian Dallas Willard, "that opens the possibility of a radical relationship to God that can withstand all external events up to and beyond death."[11]

Jesus practiced and found strength in periodic solitude. Yet today, many are frightened by solitude. Perhaps the more the idea threatens us, the more we ought to consider it. "I don't know of any answer to busyness other than solitude," says Willard. "Or tragedy."[12]

CHAPTER 4

■ ■ ■ ■ ■ ■ ■ ■

Activity and Commitment

■ Some people can't say no. They enroll in too many courses, hold down too many jobs, volunteer for too many tasks, make too many appointments, serve on too many committees, have too many friends. They are trying to be all things to all people all at once all by themselves.—DR. J. GRANT HOWARD

■ When we do two things simultaneously, we take about thirty percent of our attention off the primary task.
—RICHARD THIEME

■ It now takes twenty-to-thirty phone calls in the average church to get the same number of volunteers as it used to take two-to-three calls.—DR. JENNIFER GLASS, UNIVERSITY OF IOWA

■ God will not guide us into an intolerable scramble of panting feverishness.—THOMAS KELLY

Busy. Perhaps the primary descriptor of modern living. "Whenever two people meet today, one or the other is sure to mention how busy he or she is," observes author John Charles Cooper. "No one seems to have any free time."[1] Booked up weeks in advance, we try to do two or three things at the same time in an attempt to squeeze still more in. If in 1950 we had ten activities to choose from, today—compliments of progress—we have a thousand. Further complicating matters, most of these activities are either fun or worthy, and overload descends upon us in an avalanche.

Activity is a most excellent thing. So is commitment. It is good to be involved, vital, and energetic. On the other hand, inactivity, by its very name, connotes laziness, idleness, and lethargy.

Even activity overload can, at times, be appropriate and normal. But *chronic* activity overload is a toxic condition. Nearly every individual and family I know is afflicted.

Activity overload takes away the pleasure of anticipation. Suddenly the activity is upon us, and we must rush to it. We also lack the delight of reminiscing, for we are immediately on to new activities.

Activity overload also leads to agenda overload. People's schedules are so full that one does not often see shared agenda. Friendships which formerly were solidified by shared activities are now divided asunder by activity overload.

Activity overload also leads to exhaustion, of which we have no shortage. Consider this church's experience:

"Two summers ago, we had a schedule bordering on the insane. Besides two 'work days' each week to help construct our new sanctuary, we hosted three choir-and-mission teams, two volunteer building teams, held a week of vacation Bible school [and] two weeks of day camps, supervised two college-age summer missionaries in a full slate of youth and children's activities, and conducted two old-fashioned tent meetings.

"About all we reaped that summer was an exhausted leadership and a listless congregation for the next six months. Even our most dedicated members were peeking from behind their curtains to make sure no one was coming to recruit them for a new project."[2]

BUSYNESS, DRIVENNESS, VALUE, AND GUILT

Despite most people's abundant personal—and painful—experience with activity overload, it is interesting to see how we have normalized such a state. We have come to believe that *activity* is all that counts, everything else being sloth. If we are not busy, we are not of value. Where did this notion come from? And why is it so strongly resident within us?

The associated guilt that comes from inactivity, in turn, feeds nicely into the prevalent value system of driven people. "Driven people operate on the precept that a reputation for busyness is a sign of success and personal importance," explains Gordon MacDonald. "Thus they attempt to impress people with the fullness of their schedule. They may even express a high level of self-pity, bemoaning the 'trap' of responsibility they claim to be in, wishing aloud that there was some possible release from all that they have to live with.

But just try to suggest a way out!"[3]

In addition to the guilt of inactivity, there is an associated pride that comes from being busy. "When in high school, I prided myself on the outrageous number of extra-curricular activities I participated in," one graduate student in therapy told me. "I used to joke with people that we could get together provided they used some of my free time between 2:00-4:00 A.M." The tighter the schedule, the better driven people feel about themselves and their achievement. They often push themselves to the breaking point before realizing the danger of overload.

From a missionary who served in East Africa comes a contrasting view: "I think back to the nine years our family enjoyed on the lower slopes of the Kilimanjaro," reminisces Mildred Tengbom. "There, while our work was sometimes tense, the pace surely resembled more a walk than a run. There were plenty of green trees to sit under and a conscience that allowed us to sit down under them. We weren't constantly being told that our value depended on how 'active' or 'involved' we were."[4]

Which notion is correct? In fact, God created both activity and rest, and commends both to us. It is an essential cycle now so distantly lost it seems only ancient historians and archeologists can dig up the memory.

The Activity-Rest Cycle

As Americans, we tend to equate the will of God with busyness. But God is actually interested in both sides of the equation, and the extreme imbalance we currently live under is a fairly modern development.

Augustine talked of the active life and the contemplative life. While both had an important role to play, the contemplative life—being the domain of reflection, mediation, and prayer—was considered of greater value.[5]

If a patient has rheumatoid arthritis, in addition to important medications, two therapeutic measures are essential: activity and rest. Rheumatoid patients need daily activity or their joints will freeze up. But they also need well-defined times of rest or their joints will be destroyed.

Our lives are similar to that of the rheumatoid patient. Activity and rest. Together. Balanced. Both important. Both of God.

Even though progress will be forever giving us more and more activity, faster and faster, God is not the sponsor or supporter of this development. In the midst of it all, He wants us to find Him, to live in Him, to rest in Him. "Our heavenly Father never gives us too much to do," claims pastor and author Charles Shedd. "We assign ourselves an overload, but never the Lord."[6]

Busyness is not a synonym for kingdom work, it is only busyness. And busyness is sometimes what happens to us when we forget who God is.

PRESCRIPTIONS FOR CALMING THE ACTIVITY STORM

What steps can we take to bring balance and sanity to our hyperactive and overly committed lives?

Rx 1 *Reestablish Control of Your Life and Schedule*
Most of us are hemmed in by scores of societal influences and pressures. The first thing we need to recognize is that we have more control than we think. We should never completely relinquish our schedule to the unpredictable, commercialized, spiritually inauthentic, and sometimes ruthless whims of the world.

Be *active* in self-examination and *intentional* in correction. Abandon self-pity. Nobody is locked into anything. We *can* accomplish the needed changes if we want them badly enough. Live as simply and as slowly as needed in order to make the necessary changes.

Rx 2 *Prioritize Activities and Commitments*
Inherent in the understanding about overload is the need to prioritize. If we have more to do than we can possibly do, then we must choose. And we must choose wisely according to God-honoring criteria.

Many people do not consciously realize what their priorities are. The following are principles I have attempted to use:

■ Get priorities from the Word of God.
■ Look through God's eyes, and then act on what is seen.

■ Seek *first* the kingdom of God, and everything else *later.*
■ People are more important than things.

Rx 3 *Practice Saying NO to Good Things*

Once we clearly understand our priorities, the next step is learning how to say *no.* It is only a two-letter word and yet one of the most difficult to speak.

Regaining margin and control in our lives will never happen unless we develop the ability to say *no*—even to good things. It is easy to say *no* to bad things—like a root canal, an IRS audit, or a flexible sigmoidoscopy. But it is hard to say *no* to things we enjoy.

Practice. Stand in front of the mirror and say *no* over and over again until you get good at it. Take lessons from a two-year-old.

Saying *no* is not an excuse for noninvolvement, laziness, or insensitivity. Instead, it is purely a mechanism for living by our priorities, allowing God to direct our lives rather than the world, and preserving our vitality for the things that really matter.

One pastor told me that in his church, *no* is a holy word. Theologian Thomas Kelly encourages us to find that group of people who are so centered in the things of eternity that "*No* as well as *yes* can be said with confidence."[7]

"Bombarded with requests?" asks Dr. J. Grant Howard. "Learn to say no! Already overcommitted? Cut back! See something else that needs to be done? Delegate it!"[8]

Rx 4 *Consider Doing Less, Not More*

If most of us are already too busy, then we have some cutting back to do. Determine to do less, not more. But also determine to do the *right things*—another decision that requires a clear understanding of priorities. All activities need to be assessed for their spiritual authenticity.

The problems of the world will not be solved by our accomplishing another ten percent more in life. Consider doing ten percent *less.* Decide what is most important and concentrate on that.

Rx 5 *Protect Open Spaces*

Don't saturate your schedule. There is no need to feel guilty if your calendar has empty dates and open spaces. On the contrary, it is abnormal and unhealthy to have none. This is the precise message of margin—we need some space to heal and time to rest.

"My life in Connecticut . . . there is so little empty space," lamented Anne Morrow Lindbergh. "There are so few empty pages in my engagement pad, or empty hours in the day, or empty rooms in my life in which to stand alone and find myself. Too many activities, and people, and things. Too many worthy activities, valuable things, and interesting people. For it is not merely the trivial which clutters our lives but the important as well."[9]

Create space. Then guard it against the overloading pressures of the world at your door.

Rx 6 *Periodically Prune Activities*

Every year the apple trees in my front yard sprout new branches without even being asked. It would seem that these branches might increase the health and yield of the trees. However it is only when I actively prune away unnecessary growth that the trees flourish.

In the same way, every year our lives sprout new "activity branches"[10] without our intending it. There are always new meetings, committees, concerts, lectures, plays, parties, musicals, dinners, and sporting events that add themselves to our lives. Many activities are self-perpetuating even when we lose interest in them.

All activities, according to time management author Robert Banks, "should come up for periodic review and be required to justify their continued existence."[11] So mark your calendar, and prune on schedule.

Rx 7 *Limit Long-Term Commitments*

Since humans are limited, the number of our long-term or ongoing commitments should be limited as well. We can only spread ourselves so thin. If we are on the board of education in town, the infection control committee at the hospital, and the building committee at church, when will we find time to serve on the CPR committee for our marriage?

Rx 8 *Work to Establish and Maintain Balance*

An unexamined life will drift toward imbalance. This is the way the modern world works. And an unbalanced life will not be kind to us in the area neglected. If God has instructed us to perform in a certain area—even at the decent minimum level—then we will not thrive if we disobey.

Listen to God's advice. Take control of each area in your life where He has given explicit instructions. When we bring our balancing problems to God, we discover that He never assigns us twice as much as we can possibly do. Instead, the Father shows us the appropriate priorities to use and then always provides whatever time and resources we need to accomplish His will.

Rx 9 *Guard the Dinner Hour*

In biblical times people worked hard in the fields all day. When they came home, as darkness settled in, they reclined for the evening meal and spent hours eating and discussing. Then they went to bed.

In stark contrast, for most American families the concept of a family dinner hour has all but disappeared. We perhaps have not yet realized the magnitude of our loss.

I don't want to be a strict legalist, for it is neither practical nor possible to guard this hour rigidly. But try to establish *some* protections for the dinner hour. Try to eat at least four meals together a week. And refuse activities that would invade this time, simply because the family dinner hour is more valuable than these other commitments—no matter how valuable they might seem.

Rx 10 *Restore the Practice of Sabbath Rest*

When speaking to a group of stressed-out congressional staffers, one attractive young lady raised her hand with an unexpected and insightful question: "If we had held to the notion of a Sabbath rest, is it possible we would not be in this state of national exhaustion?"

I responded, "Yes. I think you are right. I suspect that if we unplugged one day in seven from the frenzy of the world, the amount of restedness might prove sufficiently therapeutic to spread over the rest of the week."

When our culture started to let the Sabbath slip (for example, Sunday morning soccer leagues), it was the beginning of a flood of complicating problems. In a survey of *Working Mothers* readers, ninety-five percent of people look forward to weekends to rest. But fifty-two percent were more exhausted at the end of the weekend than they were before.

Use the Sabbath both to rest from busyness and to remember God's great deeds on our behalf.

Rx 11 *Fast; Lie Fallow*

Imagine a one or two week fast—total shutdown—from activities. It would be an interesting experience. Perhaps *jarring* would be a better word. For most moderns, the experience would be so foreign that we could not tolerate it.

For the first few days, we would probably be so disoriented that we would feel the experiment is not working. As with any withdrawal there might be a nervous feeling, akin to panic. Just because it feels so uncertain is no reason that we should judge prematurely. Remember, it takes time to learn right living—just as it takes time to learn how to ride a bike or detoxify from alcohol.

Go to the mountains and lock yourself in a cabin for a week. Don't bring any electronics. Just sleep when you get tired and wake when you have slept enough.

Even a regular day away can be beneficial. "I've learned the necessity of stepping back, looking where I was going, and having a monthly quiet day to be drawn up into the mind of God," says theologian John Stott.[12]

Rx 12 *Remember Who It Is That Gets Things Done*

God is the multiplying coefficient for our labors. We might only do fifty percent of all that we had planned tomorrow and yet *accomplish* five hundred percent more in terms of eternal significance—if our efforts are sensitive to the promptings and empowerment of the Holy Spirit.

Someone has said, "God can do in twenty minutes what it takes us twenty years to do." Let's trust more and do less.

Is it busyness that moves mountains. . . or faith?

CHAPTER 5

■ ■ ■ ■ ■ ■ ■

Change and Stress

■ The only trouble with success is that the formula for achieving it is the same as the formula for a nervous breakdown.—CHUCK SWINDOLL

■ Although people will pay to fix their stress, they are not about to change the lifestyle that is causing it.
—DAVID C. MCCASLAND

■ Stress may be the spice of life or the kiss of death.
—ROBERT ELLIOT, M.D., CARDIOLOGIST

■ Things get worse under pressure.—MURPHY'S LAW OF THERMODYNAMICS

William Shakespeare was born in 1564. When he died in 1616, the world around him was not very different from the world he was born into. The occupational spectrum was the same, lifestyles were unchanged, disease and life expectancy were the same, family makeup was the same. And so it has been, from generation to generation, for century upon century, that life has been slow and static, with the most accurate descriptor being *same,* not *changing.*

But at the beginning of this century, change picked up momentum. It has continued to accelerate through the last few decades, and the acceleration is not linear but exponential. Change is like a massive tidal wave that sweeps us up and dominates us by its own independent and autonomous strength. As a direct consequence, it has given birth to an unprecedented stress epidemic that has taxed our capacity for adaptation.

For millennia, change was slow, controlled, assessable; now it convulses at warp speed. There has been more change from 1900 to present than in all of recorded history prior to 1900. And there is no deceleration in sight.

Change and stress reside together in the same equation. The key to understanding stress is understanding change.

CHANGE OVERLOAD

In the sixties, Bob Dylan alerted us to the fact that "the times, they are a-changin'." In 1970, Alvin Toffler proved it. Toffler had written other books, but it was *Future Shock* that put his name on tongues across America. The book sold millions, became an overnight classic, and was not only required reading, but required mentioning.

Toffler was concerned about not only rapid change, but more importantly, the astounding increase in the rate of change. Future Shock, maintained Toffler, is a "roaring current of change, a current so powerful today that it overturns institutions, shifts our values and shrivels our roots. Change is the process by which the future invades our lives . . . unless man quickly learns to control the rate of change in his personal affairs as well as in society at large, we are doomed to a massive adaptational breakdown."[1]

Toffler saw more clearly than Dylan. We were not merely a-changin'—we were explodin'. And, predictably, it has only increased. We no longer live in a place planted on a firm foundation but instead on an ever-shifting, ever-changing continuum of uncertainty that keeps everyone off balance.

Change has been pervasive in all areas of our society. In our personal lives, we change jobs between seven to ten times in our lifetime and careers three times. Women, on average, change jobs every 5.8 years and men every 7.6 years.[2]

We change residences even more frequently. "In the United States a man builds a house in which to spend his old age, and he sells it before the roof is on," wrote Alexis de Tocqueville in 1835. Today the average American occupies twelve or thirteen residences in the course of a lifetime, twice as many as the average person in Britain or France and four times as many as the typical Irish.[3] In a five-year period, between forty and fifty percent of Americans will change addresses. Part of this is due to the U.S. divorce rate, the highest in the world—another modern change with its own set of stressful consequences.

With job and address changes, the kids change schools and friends, while the entire family changes neighbors, churches, insurance, doctors, dentists, and grocery stores. If we don't move, our neighbors do. Even without a move, we may change doctors because of insurance mandates.

This change dynamic affects the local church also. With the average family moving once every five years and senior pastors changing churches on the average of every four years, instability ensues. Even people who don't move to a different town still change churches on average every four years. We also increasingly change church traditions. In the 1950s only four percent of church members in the average church had grown up in another denomination. By 1993, the figure had risen to forty percent.[4] And then the pew Bible is likely to change to a new translation chosen from among 450 English language versions.

The profound social and moral changes of the past half century have devastated traditions, reconfigured families, rewritten rules, and upset moral structures. The ripple effects have turned into shock waves, affecting virtually every quadrant of our social experience: governmental spending, poverty statistics, parenting and day care, birth control and sexuality, medical ethics, beginning and end of life decisions, music, movies, and television. All of which prompted historian William Manchester, when comparing 1930 with 1990, to write "One can almost say that everything that was then is not now, and everything that was not then now is."[5]

"But now we must face the fact that we all live in radically different times," explains psychiatrist Dr. Frederic Flach in his book *Resilience*. "It is one thing to go through periods of personal disruption and recovery when the world around us is relatively stable. It is quite another to have to do so when the rate at which change is taking place throughout the world has become incredibly accelerated and whole cultures find themselves on the verge of disarray. More and more, each of us is at greater risk. We have little choice but to take responsibility for weathering change very much unto ourselves."[6]

These conditions represent a change dynamic unprecedented in human history. By God's design, we were created remarkably adaptable. But adaptability has limits.

STRESS OVERLOAD

Stress is directly related to change. Three hundred years ago, people did not have much stress. Yes, they had pain, tragedy, destitution, hardship, and suffering—but they did not have much change, and therefore, by definition, they did not have much stress. Today's conditions, however, are vastly different. The flood of change sweeping over every quadrant of our existence has brought with it unprecedented stress. Vintage overload.

Stress is an internal physiologic adaptation to any change in our environment. This *stress response* was God's idea, placed within us at Creation. Despite the generally negative connotation of stress, the stress response is value neutral.

Would you like a stress-free life? If you are wise, you would not accept that option—no matter how tempting it might sound. If we do not have change, challenge, and novelty in our lives, we would literally die.

How about a *low-stress* life compared to a *high-stress* life? Surprisingly, studies reveal that most people would prefer the high-stress scenario. Having little memory of what the low-stress state feels like, most of us can't recall being bored. To remind you, it's . . . boring.

Without at least some change and stress, we languish. But if, on the other hand, there is too much change and stress, our adaptational mechanism breaks down. Because of our contemporary turbo-charged change dynamic, most of America is in a hyperstress environment.

Stress contributes to a myriad of illnesses. Some patients exhibit cardiovascular symptoms, such as racing pulse or chest pain. Some experience gastrointestinal problems such as hyperacidity, irritable bowel, or diarrhea. Some break out in rashes or develop tics. Headaches, as well as other musculoskeletal aches and pains, are common. Some people experience immunological compromise, resulting in more infections, or possibly even higher risks for cancer. Still others have insomnia, anxiety, depression. . . . The list is endless.

When stress is pushed to the extremes, burnout results. Next time you go into a forest, take a small sapling and bend it over. When you let go, the tree will straighten back up again. Now take that same sapling and bend it until it breaks. When you let go, it cannot straighten back up. This is a picture of burnout. In the same way, in our lives, we adapt and adapt and adapt—and then something inside of us snaps. When this happens, healing comes slowly. I personally do not believe we ever get back the same level of enthusiasm, innocence, and passion that we previously had. Yes, there is life after burnout. But most of the healing is by scar formation.

PRESCRIPTIONS FOR CONTROLLING CHANGE AND BLUNTING STRESS

While we cannot completely stop change or eliminate stress, there are practical steps we can take to control these areas of overload.

Rx 1 *Slow the Rate of Change*

Much of our personal change stems from broader societal trends around us, and make no mistake, these are powerful forces. Nevertheless, a significant component of every person's change index is a direct result of personal choice.

If you are stressed out, slow the rate of change. If you have been future-shocked, hunker down for a spell. Put that job decision on hold for six months. Don't move. Let the kids finish the school year. Keep your church, your pastor, your friends. If you are stressed out, you will need them more than you might think.

If you choose *not* to slow the rate of change, consider obtaining a life-change score from a counselor. A life-change index assigns points to various changes (everything from getting a pet to losing a loved one). This will allow you to quantify both the positive and negative changes in your life, each of which contribute to your overall score. If the numbers rise too high, seriously consider putting a moratorium on any significant change for six to twelve months. Otherwise, you face a high likelihood of physical or emotional illness.

Rx 2 *Move Less Often*

Make a conscious decision to sink in roots—one house, one town, one church—for one decade. Plant a one-foot-high apple tree in your yard, and don't move until it yields a bushel. Better yet, plant an acorn, and don't move until the grandchildren build a tree fort in its branches.

Not only does this slow the adaptational response—which is equivalent to stress—but it also encourages us to invest in relationships and learn to deal with issues over a longer period of time.

Also we should make note of the stress involved in building a home. Although I have not seen studies, there is plenty of anecdotal evidence. One physician's wife told me, "If your marriage can survive building a house, it can survive anything." Be forewarned.

Pastors are often called to relocate frequently. While this can be involuntary, at other times there is a prominent element of volition involved. But there is much to commend pastoral longevity in a church.

Rx 3 *Don't Overvalue Newness*

Just because something is new doesn't mean it is better. We tend to want the newest, automatically thinking it is best. Yet how often do we find some forty-year-old garden utensil at a garage sale which is more functional than the one we bought at the hardware store yesterday?

In medicine we are continuously being encouraged to try the "newest" medications. This means, however, we must now learn the dosage and side effects, and the patient has to adjust to a different regimen. Often these drugs are much more expensive and prove to be no more effective than the older, cheaper medicines we have been using for decades.

Change is sometimes improvement, but it is often pure novelty. If it adds to your stress level, see past the novelty and think twice.

Rx 4 *Establish Stability Zones*

When the only seeming constant is change, most of us can benefit from having areas in our lives where change is minimized and where stability and reliability are assured. "In the face of rapid change and over choice, a 'personal stability zone' is an important source of security and anchorage," observes stress author Walt Schafer. "A personal stability zone is any object, place, activity, belief, person, or group that is stable and constant through time, regardless of other changes."[7]

Safe havens become a valuable respite from a chaotic and otherwise unpredictable world. They can be as simple as a favorite spot for meditation or prayer, as predictable as a routine annual vacation spot, or as accepting as a long-term small group. Such friendly and comfortable points of reference become familiar harbors in stormy seas.

Rx 5 *Put More Control in Your Life*
The control issue is of central importance in determining the destructiveness of a stress experience. The first thing we should tell ourselves in any stressful situation is that we have more control over circumstances than we think. This is especially true of our *response* to the stressor. Before external stressors can make us miserable, they must first have our permission. If we can learn to rise above stressful circumstances, we will have discovered a key not only to stress, but also to spiritual maturity.

A helpful equation is $E + R = O$ (Event + Response = Outcome). You might not have control over the Event, but you do have control over the Response.

Rx 6 *Develop a Network of Caring Friends*
Studies consistently reveal a link between nurturing friendships and personal well-being. If I am hurting and go to a caring friend, empathy is in itself therapeutic. Researchers have studied what is called "the disclosure effect." If I have a frustration inside and am able to reveal my heart to a safe friend, simply "disclosing" the problem will improve my well-being in measurable ways. It is not necessary for my friend to fix the problem—all he or she has to do is listen.

Unfortunately, the rushed, stressful, marginless lifestyles so typical of modern living are toxic to friendships. It is very difficult to maintain mutual nurturing friendships in our nanosecond, change-overloaded culture.

Rx 7 *Spread Goodwill*

According to Dr. Hans Selye, the father of stress research, one of the greatest buffers against the ravages of future stress is to spread goodwill in the lives of other people. When stress comes to visit us, these people will surround us with their affirmation and support.

"Earn others' goodwill by helping them, and you will help yourself" might sound self-serving. But from another perspective, it is simply God closing His own feedback loop.

Rx 8 *Learn to Laugh*

The therapeutic benefits of laughter are well established in modern medicine as state-of-the-art, stress-reducing therapeutics. We don't yet fully understand *why* laughter works, but we do know that people who laugh heal faster.

The peak age of laughter is age four. I don't know if God is behind this symmetry, but four-year-olds laugh once every four minutes, or four hundred times a day. Adults, on the other hand, laugh fifteen times a day. If we were to follow four-year-olds around and laugh every time they do, positive things would happen to both our bodies and spirits. Laughter lowers the pulse and blood pressure and seems to improve immune functioning. One psychiatrist recommends thirty minutes of therapeutic laughter every day. Some people call this "inner jogging." Another laughter consultant calls it a cerebral enema.

The ability to laugh at oneself is perhaps most valuable. "Blessed are those who laugh at themselves, for they will never cease to be amused." In addition, laughing at our own problems has a way of putting them into perspective. One person, after a hurricane in southern Florida devastated his house, put a sign up in the front yard: "Open House." It didn't help him rebuild, but it surely helped him weather the storm.

Rx 9 *Play Music*

Seventy-five percent of Americans use music to de-stress. In response to the increasingly stressful conditions of everyday life, music therapists are emerging all across the United States. Studies reveal that surgeons who can choose their own music in the operating room have improved cardiovascular parameters during stressful surgeries. If, on the other hand, the music was chosen *for* them, there was no such benefit.

When God created music, He somehow ordained that it would be able to penetrate through superficial layers of our consciousness and go straight to the depths of our spirit. It has been my own experience, during times of significant stress, that music has helped me when nothing else could.

Find the music that ministers most precisely to your need and play it over and over. Massage your soul with a divine, supernatural balm, directly from the creative loving heart of God to yours.

Rx 10 *Rest*

"Come to me, all you who are weary and heavy burdened," offered Jesus, "and I will give you rest."[8] Just because He said this two thousand years ago doesn't mean it doesn't apply today. We can listen to culture when it says that rest is an idle waste; or we can listen to Christ when He says that rest is a divine gift. I've already cast my vote.

Rx 11 *Breathe Deeply*

Inhaling slowly, take a deep breath as you count to eight. Now, hold it for another eight seconds. Then exhale very slowly for the count of eight. This simple 8-8-8 breathing exercise is low-tech but highly effective. It forces us to slow the hurry for a brief time and to think about our breathing instead of our stress. Through physiologic mechanisms I don't fully understand, it seems to melt tension.

Rx 12 *Exercise It Away*

Many people "sweat to forget," finding it highly effective. Of course, our overloaded lives often don't allow time to exercise, and our emotional exhaustion makes it seem distinctly unappealing. But at least one study revealed a jogging program equal to antidepressants in treating depression.

Rx 13 *Stress Switch*

If engaged in a stressful activity—for example, attempting unsuccessfully to balance the checkbook—don't set it aside and lay on the couch thinking about the problem. This would penalize the mind with continued frustration. Instead practice "stress switching." Do something physical, something enjoyable. For example, I cut and stack wood or mow the lawn. I enjoy garden and lawn work and find this therapeutic. Others use sports or jogging. Even a short amount of stress switching seems to work. Any kind of diversion, representing a voluntary change of activity, is often better than inactively ruminating on the stressor.

Rx 14 *Limit Your Time with Negative People*
Negative people can be draining and one of life's greatest stressors. They usually do not want to get well. No matter how much you invest in them, they often do not improve.

It is a good idea—and a healthy exercise of boundaries—to limit time with such people. If you nevertheless feel you want to reach out to them, please do so. But be careful. Don't be naive. Attempting to "rescue" such people often does not objectively improve their life, it only exhausts yours.

Rx 15 *Don't Worry*
Most of us realize that worry is senseless. The saying "Worry does not empty tomorrow of its troubles—it only empties today of its strength" is succinct and fully accurate.

Beyond this commonsense knowledge, we now realize that worry can be medically harmful. A recent study in the medical journal *Circulation* reveals that people who had increased measurements of worry have poorer health outcomes.[9]

Jesus advised, "Do not worry about tomorrow for tomorrow will worry about itself. Each day has enough trouble of its own."[10] Even though many believers have heard this verse for decades, nevertheless they freely worry as if the Bible were silent. How strange it has not occurred to us that such worry is sin! "I had to learn that worry is sin," confesses Corrie ten Boom, "before I could get rid of the worry."[11]

Rx 16 *Reduce Stress*
Many books and seminars emphasize *stress management*. This is an important concept to teach, as we can blunt the ill-effects of stress

by changing our reaction to stressors. Certainly our *perception* of the event matters a great deal, and our *response* to that perception matters even more. As was written even in ancient times: "Men are distressed not by things, but by the views which they take of them."

However, it is also important to recognize that if we live in a hyperstressed environment, *reducing* stress is just as important as managing it. Those who suggest our total approach should be "management" are not being realistic. If living in extraordinarily stressful circumstances day-in and day-out, the sanest thing a person could do is to change the circumstances, not just adapt.

Rx 17 *Problem Solved*

Even though God did not give Christians a magical stress exemption, He did remove forever the most important stressor in the universe. When we are feeling overwhelmed, it is good to remember that our biggest problem—larger than all the problems in the world added together and multiplied by infinity—was solved at the Cross. Forever. Freely.

"In the world you will have tribulation," said Jesus. "But be of good cheer; I have overcome the world."[12]

CHAPTER 6

■ ■ ■ ■ ■ ■ ■

Choice and Decision

■ The right to choose is as American as apple pie (or pumpkin pie, or Boston cream pie, or pecan pie).
—ROBERT KANIGEL

■ One of the tenacious paradoxes of technology is that we have more choices, but less time to choose.
—EDWARD WENK, JR.

■ We are, in fact, racing toward "overchoice."
—ALVIN TOFFLER

■ While incarcerated prisoners make twenty decisions a day, those of us walking the streets make one hundred and twenty decisions a day.—PRISON FELLOWSHIP

While writing *Margin* in the early 1990s, I rented a winter cabin in the lonely Wisconsin north woods. In a fortress guarded by snow and cold I would frequently spend two weeks at a time there, writing nights and sleeping days. During that creative interlude I came to appreciate the solitude and simplicity of rustic living.

When it came time to buy supplies, the tiny town of Birchwood was my only destination. The grocery store was a small, spotless IGA with hardwood floors and few customers. I grew to love that store and its clean simplicity. While the average supermarket today swells with thirty thousand different products, this IGA perhaps had fewer than two thousand. But I needed only five, maybe ten. Why wander miles of aisles?

The store had six choices of cereal. Not hard choices—I was satisfied with any of them. Back home I curiously inventoried the cereal variety available at our family grocery: 184 different kinds. Even when I knew the specific cereal I wanted, it still took time to find it amidst so many competing varieties and sizes.

That small rural grocery illustrated for me a valuable lesson: Just because we have increased choice does not automatically mean we have increased benefit. If choice is a freedom, it can also be a burden. Yet the breadth of choices will only continue to proliferate. "Ironically, the people of the future may suffer not from an absence of choice, but from a paralyzing surfeit of it," explained Alvin Toffler. "They may turn out to be victims of that peculiarly super-industrial dilemma: overchoice . . . the point at which the advantages of diversity and individualization are canceled by the complexity of the buyer's decision-making process."[1]

Writer Robert Kanigel understands about such overload and limits. "Here's the problem: While choices multiply, we stay pretty much the same. Our bodies and minds remain the bottleneck through which choice must pass. We still have the same brains our forebears did, still only twenty-four hours a day to use them. We still need time and energy to listen, look, absorb, distinguish, and decide. The opportunity to choose among many options is, of course, a good thing. But maybe you can have too much of a good thing? Even of choice itself? . . . Each choice saps energy, takes time, makes a big deal out of what isn't."[2]

So much of daily living is now involved with the making of trivial decisions based on this incredible profusion of choice. As Thoreau wrote in *Walden,* "Our life is frittered away by detail."

To illustrate, here are some statistics compiled over the past fifteen years researching societal trends. Some are very current, others perhaps not. Nevertheless, they accurately convey the magnitude of the problem involved in contemporary choice and decision overload.

> 55 medical specialties
> 60 different kinds of Muzak ("elevator music")
> 80 different blood pressure medicines
> 93 brands of bottled water at an Amsterdam
>   boutique
> 125 kinds of yogurt
> 126 different types of subcompact cars
> 177 kinds of salad dressing

184 kinds of breakfast cereal

249 kinds of soap

250 kinds of toothpaste

450 English language versions of the Bible

500 different bachelor's degrees being offered in
college

551 kinds of coffee

752 different models of cars and trucks sold in the
U.S.

1,200 new business books every year

1,500 movies per month to choose from with a satellite dish

1,500 insurance payers in the American system

2,500 types of light bulbs—in one store alone

3,000 different medications in the Physician's Desk
Reference

4,500 new children's books every year

5,000 magazines to choose from

30,000 different products in the average grocery store

58,000 new books or new editions every year

` 1,000,000 titles from Barnes & Noble on-line

25,000,000 different versions of automobiles when all possible combinations of styles, options, and colors
available are taken into account

Missionaries returning from abroad routinely comment on the staggering and almost gluttonous selection of goods and services available in American stores. For example, Oreo cookies—now you can buy mint, double stuff, chocolate dipped, giant, or regular. I don't remember any crescendo of discontent responsible for this new proliferation.

Toothpaste is available in 250 different varieties. As I approached the Crest display recently, I found not only regular but also mint, gel, kid's gel, tartar control regular, tartar control gel—all in both pumps and tubes, not to mention a multitude of sizes.

Milk now comes in whole milk, reduced-fat milk, low-fat milk, non-fat milk, buttermilk, acidophilus milk, calcium-fortified milk, soy milk (plain), lactaid, goat's milk, carbonated milk, and milk with juice. And ice cream? . . . the hundreds of flavors include avocado and shrimp. "Recently, I was in an ice-cream parlor in San Francisco that served the sort of fresh-fruit drinks sometimes called smoothies," observes columnist Calvin Trillin, "and I noticed that the add-ins you could get in your smoothie (most of them for an extra fifty cents) were listed as follows: *spirulina, bee pollen, brewer's yeast, calcium, ginseng, lecithin, protein powder mix, vitamins & minerals, and wheat germ.* In Kansas City, people would pay a lot more than fifty cents to have any of those things removed from whatever they were eating and replaced with Betty Lucas' chicken batter."[3] Obviously, not everyone has the same tastes—part of the reason for choice I suppose.

On top of this are the 327 *billion* discount coupons published annually in the U.S. People now wander through their ultra-mega-supermarket, purses and pockets stuffed with coupons, with little thought that their minutes and hours are increasingly being consumed by the trivialities of modern commercialism. Personally, I can think of better ways to invest my time than browsing among thirty kinds of toilet paper.

DECISION STRESS AND PROGRESS

Where did this mountainous avalanche of choice come from? "The most fundamental reason we moderns are plagued with an overabundance of choices," explains sociologist S. D. Gaede, "is that we are a choice-seeking people. We want more alternatives, more options, more possibilities."[4]

His observation is true, yet there is a deeper reason: progress. As we have already seen, progress works by differentiating our environment, automatically giving us more and more, faster and faster. Progress relentlessly results in choice. And *choice* requires *decision.*

"Because of the rapidity of change occurring in our society . . . leaders are faced with the need to make more decisions than ever, and to make them more quickly than was expected previously," observe researchers George Barna and William Paul McKay.[5] Not only have decisions proliferated, but the context of the decisions is often more burdensome. It is one thing to decide whether to get rippled barbecue chips or unrippled sour cream and onion; it is entirely another to decide to unplug the respirator of a loved one.

The simple decisions don't cost us much, and we make them easily: "I'll have a Big Mac, fries, and a Coke." But modernity has brought us new choices which are not so easy: whether to have children and how many; whether to buy a house and how big a mortgage to assume; whether to move and how often; whether to change jobs; whether to change churches; whether both spouses should work outside the home or not; whether to put Grandpa into the nursing home.

The psychic stress associated with decision overload contributes much to our exhaustion. In medicine, we encounter it daily. Some days I come home from the clinic so fatigued that I crawl into the house. "What should we have for dinner?" Linda asks. "I don't know and I can't afford to think about it," I say. "I'll eat the silverware . . . the china. But please don't ask me to make another decision."

In 1947, the first *Physician's Desk Reference* (PDR) contained three hundred pages. Fifty years later it has swollen to nearly three thousand pages. How does one choose from the scores of anti-hypertensives or the hundreds of antibiotics?

One year, I received 461 invitations to medical conferences. One conference I attended in Anaheim listed over three hundred workshops or events to choose from in three days. Six months later, I attended another conference in San Diego where, again in three days, I had 511 options for involvement. It seems I spent half my time there trying to decipher the conference brochure.

ANALYSIS OVERLOAD

Choices require decisions. And decisions require analysis. The increased analytical burden required by choice and decision over-load appeared on our psychological agenda almost overnight. Yet even if analysis overload sneaked up on us and remains largely unidentified, it nevertheless results in enough daily complexity to cross a rabbi's eyes. Sales, payment options, fast food menus, IRS rules, administrative decisions, computer software. . . . Choices must first be analyzed and understood before they can be decided.

For example, AT&T (or Sprint or MCI) sends an advertisement proposing a new way to save money by reconfiguring my long distance service. It sounds good. It looks good. But is it? Really? Who knows. And even though I have a physics degree and have won math awards, I do not have the capacity to investigate. Why does AT&T want to save me money anyway? Money currently going to their pocket they now wish to switch to my pocket? Right.

When paying his phone bill, Leonard Laster, M.D., was struck with the same problem. Suspecting he was paying more than the advertised rates, he called the company to check. The woman who answered informed him he was free to investigate their various plans and choose the one that best suited his usage pattern. "When I told her that my postgraduate training in analytical mathematics was inadequate to meet such a challenge, she said that if I wished, she would enter my billing data into a computer program and perform the analysis for me. I said that I wished, and before long she determined that I had been overpaying for some time.

"She transferred my account to a more appropriate plan, and made a 'courtesy adjustment.' . . . I attempted to explore with her — but got nowhere — why the company hadn't alerted me to this situation earlier, and why the burden of the cost-benefit analysis had been covertly shifted on to my rather meager decision-making capabilities."

Following that encounter, Laster began reflecting on the growing number of analytical assignments required by the routine activities of daily living. "Are you off to lunch in a fast-food restaurant? You will be confronted with an array of menu packages — a hamburger, drink, and dessert at one price; french fries and chicken dish, with or without dessert, at another. You will have to determine the most financially effective buy, but not to worry: a simple multi-factorial variable systematic analysis will point you in the optimal direction."[6]

Analysis overload — from credit card deals to catalog sales to travel promotionals — has become an integral part of living in a choice-overloaded world. "How can you sort through preschools,

HMOs, retirement plans, or roofing contractors with equanimity intact?" asks Kanigel. "Each present difficult choices, riddled with complexities, uncertainties, places to go wrong. Maybe you're smart. And maybe you're well-educated. But you can't have a Ph.D. in *everything.*"[7]

A soloist once gave a concert in our church, and just before the break, announced that tapes would be available for six dollars each, or three for twenty dollars. No one laughed. Probably no one had the energy to do the math.

PRESCRIPTIONS FOR EASING CHOICE OVERLOAD AND DECISION STRESS

We cannot escape: choices requiring decisions requiring analysis are here to stay. Some simplifying principles, however, will help ease the distress and confusion along the way.

Rx 1 *Simplify Your Decision Making*

Decide to limit choices rather than continuously expand them. Why buy more clothes, for example, when you already have an abundant choice?

When I got tired of deciding what to wear to the office each day, I settled on a simplicity-based solution: either brown or blue pants, and either a white or blue shirt. Everything matched, and I could get dressed in the dark.

Similarly, when traveling, I have a "speaking uniform": gray slacks, a blue shirt, and a blue blazer. I don't own a suit. Einstein, it seems, owned several outfits exactly the same. On his way to discovering relativity, he did not wish to waste time deciding among trivialities.

Rx 2 *Simplify Meal Choices*

During college, I studied in Switzerland for a year, living with a Swiss physician's family. Although enjoying the highest standard of living in the world, it was interesting to witness how simply the Swiss often chose to live compared to the average American family.

Take mealtime. Every morning, we had plain homemade yogurt and dense German bread . . . the kind that if it fell off the table, it would break your foot. For the evening meal, we had the same dense bread with cheese or jam.

For the noon meal, we all sat leisurely around the dinner table for two hours (the phone never rang, and they did not own a television), while my Swiss mother served the meal. She prepared and rotated only six or seven menus. Why have more? We loved each of the options she provided.

There is no need to have fifty different kinds of foods. Decide on a dozen or so that the family really enjoys, and then stick with this routine until it is time to change. Remember, most of the world eats the same thing three times a day—and prefers it that way.

A pediatrician from Alabama wrote me after working short-term in an impoverished Central American clinic. One of her routine habits was to ask children their favorite thing to eat. Every child gave the same answer: food.

"Plan meals with your family's likes and dislikes in mind," write authors Mimi Wilson and Mary Beth Lagerborg, "but once you've set the menu, try this rule: Today's Menu—Two Choices: *Take It or Leave It.*"[8]

Rx 3 *Develop Enjoyable Routines*

Routines can, at times, be boring. But they can also be comforting or even delightful. For example, many people have an established routine for Saturday or Sunday morning breakfast. To simplify our Sunday mornings when the boys were growing up, we would have "Sunday cereal" each week—a more expensive kind of cereal that the boys enjoyed. It would vary, depending on what was on sale. But it was always something they looked forward to. And it simplified that busy morning for the entire family.

Most people drive to work over the same route each day, use the same parking spot, buy gas from the same store, and shop for groceries the same day every week.

Some people have hamburgers every Wednesday or fish every Friday. Some buy donuts every Saturday morning, have pot roast every Sunday dinner, or bake stollen every Christmas.

These routines might not add spice to life, but they do add a much needed and pleasurable *stability*. These routines are called programmed decisions, and they cut down greatly on decision stress. The vast majority of our daily decisions are "programmed" in a healthy way. Routines work.

Rx 4 *Make Decisions and Stick with Them*

Making decisions costs us in both time and energy. There is seldom a compelling reason to revisit the decision frequently. If you have decided against cable, don't redecide weekly. If you decide not to attend R-rated movies, then stick with it. If your insurance costs too much, then research the options and make an informed decision. But not quarterly — that's too much decision stress.

We have already seen how fasting, twentieth-century style, can play an important role in addressing overload. Consider fasting from choices for a period, to better concentrate on the deeper truths of life. One of the purposes of fasting is to concentrate on the transcendent. Consider shutting down the trivial to give depth a chance.

Rx 5 *Value Traditions*

Traditions are called traditions precisely because they form a link to the past. One value of tradition is that it is a celebration of sameness, not change. And when you do not change, you do not have to make a choice. "The value of a tradition is that it obviates the need for a decision," explains sociologist S. D. Gaede. "We need them because a life empty of tradition is a life void of its past and incapable of producing a meaningful future. It is a life of impoverished freedom."[9]

Identify those traditions in your personal, family, and church life that have special significance and protect them vigorously. There is nothing shameful about *old-fashioned* if the tradition represents a rich heritage and contains vital connections to the past. We need only to remember the festivals and remembrances instituted by God to understand that "sameness," in the opinion of the Almighty, can be a valuable anchor for the soul.

Rx 6 *Be Wary of Advertisements*

All ads should come with a disclaimer: "Caution: Faulty logic ahead." Ads are not trying to be helpful; they are trying to be convincing. Ads will complicate, not simplify, your decisions. And they will bias you toward purchases you will later regret. When making choices, trust your own judgment.

Rx 7 *Ignore Marketing Gimmicks*

If a company is encouraging you to reconfigure your current service or try a new one, ask yourself one simple question: Why? Once you understand the answer, your decision making is made simple.

Forget it. Don't even go through the math. Be assured that *they* have already done their math and it comes out advantageous for them.

Maybe I've grown cynical. But it simplifies my choices, my decisions, my analysis, and my life to simply ignore marketing gimmicks.

Rx 8 *Keep "Good Enough" over "Better"*

We often decide against something simply because fashion dictates tell us it is outmoded. Carpet, curtains, clothes. Why place the extra burden of decision upon us in this arena when we should perhaps be saving our strength for those decisions of greater import?

Unless they are really important to you, forget about the bells and whistles. Do we really need that new car simply because it has a new option? Or that new computer—when our current computer has fifty times more power then we will ever need? Even Microsoft, in an advertisement, claims, "Think about how many features you have in all of your software. Hundreds of them just waiting to do your bidding. If only you knew how to use them all. Because if you're like most busy people, you simply haven't got time to learn every feature in every program." Therefore, they reason, buy this Microsoft Office Upgrade.

My answer: Thanks, but what I have is already "good enough."

Rx 9 *Look Beyond the Glitter*

It is hard in the midst of a ricocheting life to choose the best things, the right things—they don't glitter as much on the surface. We eat what tastes sweetest at the time, not what ultimately digests the healthiest. There is the immediate and then the delayed—and in choosing the immediate we often sacrifice the wisdom of choosing what is best for the delayed.

When young physicians ask advice about choosing their future practice locations, I advise them to look beyond the honeymoon. The first six months of practice seems great, no matter where you go. But far more important is the first six years. "The validity of a decision is best judged on the basis of long-term consequences," observes engineer Edward Wenk, Jr. But under stress, he goes on to warn, we tend to discount the future.[10]

Decide with the future in view. You will want to live there someday.

Rx 10 *Choose Appropriate Load, Not Overload*

Although people don't always regard it as such, choosing too much to be involved in is indeed a choice. Yes, culture is responsible for much of the overload that is swamping us. But we can choose to create a margin if we want it badly enough. All it takes is a sufficient amount of counter-cultural intent.

Remember: When we insist on living overloaded lives, this choice not only damages our own well-being, but also inflicts damage on those around us.

Rx 11 *Own Your Decisions*

Many people bemoan how trapped they are in life: the boss expects too much, the family demands too much, the debts mount too fast. But ultimately we live in a world of our own choosing—even if we don't "feel" like the choice is ours. "The loss of felt choice is an everyday experience," explains psychologist Larry Crabb. "But we must state clearly that loss of *felt* choice does not mean loss of *actual* choice."[11]

"We who lived in the concentration camps can remember the men who walked through the huts comforting others, giving away their last piece of bread," recalls the late Viktor Frankl, in perhaps his most famous quotation. "They may have been few in number, but they offer sufficient proof that everything can be taken from a man but one thing: the last of his freedoms — to choose one's attitude in any given set of circumstances, to choose one's own way."

Ultimately, we are emotionally healthier and relationally happier if we own our choices. "One's philosophy is not best expressed in words. It is expressed in the choices one makes," observed former First Lady Eleanor Roosevelt. "And the choices we make are ultimately our responsibility."

Rx 12 *Pray for Wisdom in Decision Making*

We should probably pray for *all* the decisions in our lives, small or large. But at least, as a first step, we need to pray more for the important decisions, those requiring resources beyond our understanding. God promises wisdom for those who ask and trust.[12] Many times we lack this wisdom simply because we do not pray for it.[13]

I once saw a banner on the back of a church where I was speaking that stopped me in my tracks: "A life without prayer is a boast against God." Not a wise way to make decisions.

Rx 13 *Daily Re-choose the Things of God*

Just before he died, Moses reminded people of the need to choose carefully, for much is at stake. "This day I call heaven and earth as witnesses against you that I have set before you life and death, blessing and curses. Now choose life, so that you and your children may live, and that you may love the LORD your God, listen to his voice, and hold fast to him."[14]

Joshua, following Moses, declared his choice: "But if serving the LORD seems undesirable to you then choose for yourselves this day whom you will serve. . . . But as for me and my house, we will serve the LORD."[15]

Do we daily choose righteousness? Haddon Robinson talks about a "glad surrender" to the things of God. God, it seems, owns it all anyway. Our time belongs to God. So does our money. So do our careers and our possessions. Our families belong to God, we belong to God, our future belongs to God.

Only the choice belongs to us.

CHAPTER 7

■■■■■■■■

Debt

- We will loan you enough money to get you completely out of debt.—SIGN IN A LOAN OFFICE

- More than a billion people around the world live on less than a dollar a day.—RON SIDER

- Interest works night and day, in fair weather and in foul. It gnaws at a man's substance with invisible teeth.
  —HENRY WARD BEECHER

- There are two times in a man's life when he should not speculate—when he cannot afford it, and when he can.
  —MARK TWAIN

Economics has gained a dominant ascendancy over the affairs of the human race in a very short time, staggering even economic thinkers. For millennia, people were destitute, but largely self-sufficient in their destitution. If they needed a house, they built it. If they needed clothes, they made them. If they wanted bread, they baked it. Even at the time of the Revolutionary War, when ninety-two percent of Americans earned their living on the farm, independence and rugged individualism were the rule of the day. But in the same year the United States declared its independence, Adam Smith published his treatise on *The Wealth of Nations* and the world changed forever.

Smith, the father of modern economic science, taught that *free enterprise* was a higher state of historical evolution than was *government-constrained enterprise*. In this laissez-faire capitalism, humans "naturally" seek self-betterment through the economic system. As forces of competition are played out in the marketplace, an "invisible hand" translates the entire process into benefit for all by adjusting costs, goods, and labor.

In reaction to the unemployment and the Great Depression in the 1930s, John Maynard Keynes deviated from Smith's laissez-faire by urging governments to take a more active role in helping to regulate the economy, especially to reverse downturns. This led to the notion that it is acceptable for borrowing and credit to fuel such economic interventions. With such thinking in place, the U.S. national debt began to grow in the 1930s, followed by corporate debt in the 1940s. Shortly thereafter, personal debt began to swell, and by the mid-1980s, our international trade balance turned negative for the first time since 1917.

Today, our lives are addictively intertwined in the economic system, and the credit-debt mentality has been fully normalized. "Someone has described a modern American," wrote pastor and college president Paul Billheimer, "as a person who drives a bank-financed car over a bond-financed highway on credit card gas to open a charge account at a department store so he can fill his Savings and Loan financed home with installment-purchased furniture."[1]

This economic ascendancy has seen remarkable successes but equally vexatious problems. In 1997, for example, health care costs for the first time exceeded one trillion dollars—$3,759 for each person in the U.S. Health care economist Paul Starr observes that from 1948 to 1990, the amount businesses paid for health care increased fifteen and six tenths percent per year—clearly not sustainable. Health care has become so costly that millions of self-employed workers are paying as much as eight thousand dollars per family annually for coverage, and more than forty million Americans have no insurance at all.

College tuition represents a second economic predicament, rising at double the rate of inflation and increasing far faster than median family income. Today, only one out of thirteen families can afford to pay full college costs.[2] Home costs are yet another large ticket item. Even with the market correction in some regional areas, we have never recovered from the huge real estate run-up in the 1970s and 1980s.

On top of this, our consumptive notion of the Good Life has dug another debt hole. Even though eighty-two percent of Americans believe "most of us buy and consume far more than we need,"[3] the vast majority of us haven't attempted to modify our earn-and-spend lifestyles. We work harder to pay for the American Dream's debt, and even with two wage earners in the marketplace, a larger number are falling farther behind.

DEBT

Consumer debt currently stands at 1.4 trillion dollars. The amount of debt households must service has grown to its highest share of income in twenty years.[4] Still, with America awash in available cash, financial institutions are encouraging easy credit. Even though some of these loans will default, the profits from the good loans off-set the bad.

We are witnessing a fundamental restructuring of the economic system, borne primarily by the middle class, and people are using credit for types of debt they previously used banks and cash for. Easy borrowing is now so available and people's debt levels so high that many are accessing the credit market for daily expenses. "In the past, families would borrow to buy a car or send kids to college. Today, they're borrowing to gas up the car or send kids to the pediatrician," observe journalists Karen Gullo and Vivian Marino.[5]

Recently a new—and even more worrisome—credit marketing strategy has emerged: the one-hundred and twenty-five percent loan. It allows borrowers to take out a second mortgage which, when combined with the first, can total as much as one-hundred and twenty-five percent of a home's approved value. "For consumers who own homes it's one more way to keep spending," observes economist Maury Harris.[6] Consumers are, in turn, using this borrowed money to pay off credit-card debt, lower monthly mortgage payment (due to longer maturity and lower finance charges), and to provide still *more* buying power. "These risky loans break the time-honored mortgage-lending standards that require banks to lend no more than eighty percent of a home's appraised value," explains *The Wall Street Journal's* Fred R. Bleakley. "History shows that a telltale sign that an economic expansion is nearing its end occurs when lenders start making riskier loans."[7]

One consequence of our mountainous debt is a resurgence of

pawn shops. Twenty-nine million people frequent eleven thousand pawn shops across the U.S. Rather than offering the traditional thirty percent of an item's value in pawn, the new philosophy is to offer fifty percent. The profit comes not by reselling the item, but by repeat customers (increasingly well-to-do) willing to pay twenty-five percent monthly interest charges.

Financial adviser Russ Crosson teaches that, aside from the spiritual implications, debt is unwise for at least two reasons: it is three times as hard to get out of debt as to get into it, and it sentences us to a lower lifestyle in the future. Yet, aside from these individual and family concerns over debt stress, there is a growing systemic concern that this amount of consumer debt will deepen the next recession. Can this debt-sponsored credit gamble pay off indefinitely? "Given a choice between building your business on large debt or facing a firing squad . . . choose the firing squad," advises businessman and author John Capozzi. "There's a chance the firing squad might miss."[8]

CREDIT CARD PUSHERS AND USERS

A huge shift in the debt-credit strategy over the past twenty years has come through the widespread use of credit cards. Up to eighty percent of the population holds at least one major credit card. More than one *billion* are burning holes in wallets and purses in the United States. Yet, even with this level of saturation, 2.5 billion new credit card offers are mailed each year. Each individual receives, on average, twenty offers per year.

Today, we can obtain specialty cards not only through our banks, department stores, gas stations, and phone companies, but also from our union, grocery store, and on-line service. The Association of Trial Lawyers has a card, as do fans of Frank Sinatra. Even sixty-two percent of college students have credit cards.

Meanwhile, reflective of our deeper consumer debt, credit-card debt is doubling every five years and credit-card delinquencies are at the highest level in twenty-four years. Even though only two or three out of one hundred accounts will default, only one in three accounts pay off the balance each month.

One man had twenty credit cards all charged to their limits, and yet was holding on to twenty more "just in case." Even when people go bankrupt, they still receive several credit-card solicitations every month. Some even come preapproved.

BANKRUPTCY

With such easy credit and high levels of debt, it comes as no surprise that we are setting bankruptcy records. In 1996 and again in 1997, we surpassed one million bankruptcies, each a new record. At more than twenty thousand families per week, this is a rate greatly exceeding the Great Depression. In the Great Depression, one out of every 215 people filed for bankruptcy. But if current trends hold, as many as ten percent of America's one hundred million households will declare bankruptcy in the 1990s.

How did this trend pick up such momentum? "The battle to save people from going headlong into debt was lost decades ago when lending shifted to a reliance on income rather than on assets as collateral," explains a *Forbes* article. "This democratization of credit helped fuel the growth of the economy, but it let many people get ever deeper in the credit hole."[9] When asked how people go bankrupt, author Ernest Hemingway easily answered, "Two ways: gradually, then suddenly."

Bankruptcy is largely a white, middle-class problem. Though the popular bankruptcy image is of an undisciplined spendthrift, in fact most bankruptcies are triggered by serious career, marriage, or health problems. The average bankruptcy filer is thirty-something, divorced, with one year of college, and an annual income of around $40,000.

Some say that bankruptcy has followed divorce and illegitimacy in being destigmatized, and we ought to put more shame back into it. Others blame bankruptcy lawyers, with their *Solve your debt problems quick and easy!!* ads. "Bankruptcy has become the latest entitlement in this country," complains MasterCard economist Lawrence Chimerine—not exactly an unbiased observer.[10] Others say that it is not so simple. The average bankrupt person has debt (excluding home mortgages) equal to twice his or her yearly income. And the experience still hurts. How would you like to lose the hundred-year-old family farm on your generational shift?

PRESCRIPTIONS FOR DEFEATING DEBT OVERLOAD

If culture has one hand around your wallet and another around your throat, these prescriptions will help loosen the grip.

Rx 1 *Commit to a Budget*

For anyone experiencing difficulty with debt, particularly chronic debt, the first step is to set up a budget. The scope of this book does not permit details about budgetary techniques and procedure. There are several excellent and practical books in this area, and I would recommend those by Larry Burkett or Ron Blue and Co.

Before you can set up a budget, you need to know where and how you are spending money. Start now by recording all expenses and retaining all receipts for three months.

Rx 2 *Avoid Future Debt*

The first rule of holes is this: When you are in one, stop digging. Resist the consumptive lifestyle. Say *no* to new purchases. Avoid impulse buying. Don't even go to stores, especially malls. Throw away catalogs. Don't buy now and pay later.

Relax—it isn't so bad. According to studies, "Eighty-six percent of those Americans who have voluntarily cut back their consumption say they are happier as a result."[11]

Rx 3 *Pay Off Debt Systematically*

Make a plan, and stick to it. One idea consists of a four-step process: First, list all debts in order, from the smallest to the largest. Be sure everything is included. Second, make sure to pay at least the minimum payment on each debt each month. Third, double payments on the debt at the top of the list whenever possible. Fourth, as each debt is paid off, apply that payment plus the minimum payment toward the next debt.

Rx 4 *Dispose of Credit Cards*

If you have a debt problem, chances are fairly good that you also have a credit-card problem. If credit cards control you, control them instead. Cut them up and throw them away. Have a ceremony and burn them in the fireplace. Don't try to "modify" credit-card habits, as it often doesn't work. The best approach is cold turkey.

Rx 5 *Develop an Accountability Network*

Any lifestyle change is greatly assisted if an accountability structure is involved. We all cheat on ourselves. But when we bring in the spotlight of scrutiny from another objective person, many of our rationalizations wilt. Find another person or a group and discuss expenditures at least once a week.

Rx 6 *Examine Your Motives for Spending*

What is your psychology of spending? If we better understood why we spend, it will bring us halfway home in our quest for freedom from debt. There are many different motives, not all of which we care to confront. Do we spend because we simply enjoy buying? Do we spend when depressed? When bored? Are we addicted? Do we attempt to buy our way into the hearts of others? Do we buy because of peer pressure from those around us? . . . those at work? . . . those at church? . . . those in our neighborhood? If we own forty pairs of shoes or six automobiles, there is something beneath the surface that needs to be understood before it can be corrected.

Rx 7 *Make Spending Need-based*

If we are honest, only a small minority of our purchases are need-based. Instead, most of our purchases are desire-based, interest-based, pleasure-based, or cash-flow based. Just because we get a raise or a hefty tax refund is no reason to increase spending.

To make certain something is a *need*, don't buy on first pass. Wait. Think about it for a day or a week. Pray about it. If it is a clear need, there will be no ambiguity. But if it is instead a desire, another desire will arise to take its place, thus clarifying the true status of need versus desires.

Rx 8 *Develop Self-sufficiency*
In comparison to previous eras, today we are neither independent nor self-sufficient. We know how to make money—but that is all. When our money-making capacity is threatened or taken away, we must borrow for every aspect of daily living. Our assault on debt will be aided by learning to do for ourselves.

Learn to change your own oil. Grow some of your own food. Sew some of your own clothes. Learn to cut hair. Linda has done this for our family for decades, saving us thousands of dollars and hundreds of hours.

Rx 9 *Integrate Lifestyle Simplicity and Contentment*
Getting out of debt is one thing; staying out is a separate matter entirely. Deeply integrating lifestyle simplicity and contentment is helpful in countering our culturally normalized debt mentality. If we are content with the things God freely gives us, expecting little and rejoicing in whatever comes our way, debt loses its fangs.

"Although less income may result in more financial pressures . . . ," observes Russ Crosson, "income is often not the reason for financial pressures; lifestyle is. Therefore, control your lifestyle, live within your income, and be content in the vocation God has called and equipped you for."[12]

This message is not an easy one. But be encouraged that millions of Americans are discovering such a newfound counter-cultural freedom. Scripture warns us to avoid conformity to the world and entanglement with its affairs.[13] Burdensome debt is in violation of these commands; biblical simplicity and contentment help set things right.

Rx 10 *Move Down*
Many people take on home mortgages that deprive them of financial margin for decades. To make payments, they overwork. Exhaustion coupled with high debt creates interpersonal problems.

Consider moving to a smaller home. Obviously, this is an important decision that should be made with care and consensus. But for some, it will solve most—or all—of their debt problems overnight.

Rx 11 *Let Appliances Die in Your Arms*

Appliances often wear out in a predictable pattern, yet other times they prove astoundingly resilient. My father, a heating and air conditioning contractor, once commented that it's frustrating when people delay replacing an old furnace until it fails in the middle of the night in the middle of a snowstorm in the middle of the winter. I gently reminded him of the clothes dryer he replaced because it was "on its last legs." Still in medical training, we willingly took the dryer off his hands—and it gave us an additional fourteen years of service. "That," I suggested, "is probably why people don't want to pay for a new furnace when the old one might have some life in it."

Rx 12 *Stop Venerating Automobiles*

If we were to examine the issue honestly, most people pay more for automobiles than is necessary and the resultant auto loans play a significant role in their overall debt picture. I wonder—how much would Jesus pay for a car?

Personally, in our family we have never paid more than $4,000 for an automobile. Obviously, if you are not careful you can get some regrettable vehicles. But mostly, we have had reliable, adequately appealing cars that are satisfactory in every way.

One person reported he sold his favorite collector's car after hearing me speak. Quite frankly, hearing such reports is distressing, because I don't want responsibility for other people's decisions. When I expressed this view, he responded, "But you don't realize how great it feels to get out from under some of our debt load. It's wonderful!"

Rx 13 *Simplify Your Meals; Eat Out Less*

Expensive grocery bills are partly required and partly chosen. If you could discipline your taste buds to accept simplicity, you would eat healthier while spending a fraction of your usual food budget. Double your rice portion and cut your meat portion in half. Your wallet will thank you; your body will too.

In addition to high grocery bills, a large number of us eat out regularly. It is a common, delectable, and socially sanctioned experience. But it is also expensive and unhealthy. In the interest of health and debt reduction, eat in.

Rx 14 *Shop for Good Deals*

If we can slow down the treadmill and not have to buy our way out of hurriedness, it becomes much easier to look for sales and bargains. Decide not to pay full price unless necessary. Realize that not all purchases need to be new—buying at thrift shops, garage sales, and Goodwill has eased financial burdens for millions.

At our house, we keep a "gift box." When we find something on sale, we make the purchase and put it in the box as a future gift. This way we buy good gifts at less price and less hassle. Once on our way to a bookstore, we passed a children's close-out sale. Linda bought three hundred dollars worth of children's clothes for thirty dollars.

Simplicity author Paul Borthwick suggests that we remember the bargain shopper's motto: "*Everything* will eventually go one sale." But he also cautions, "Discount outlets and bargain basements can be a blessing and a curse." On one hand, they sell for less, reducing our costs. On the other hand, bargains can create a destructive, materialistic attitude by leading to many unnecessary purchases.[14]

Rx 15 *Simplify Christmas and Birthdays*

Because other people are involved, making the decision to cut costs in celebrations and gift giving is a difficult one. Within your family, if your children are small, begin the process early. Explain the real meaning of gift giving, and do not let it slide into commercialism. Put thought and love into the occasion more than money. One family set a limit—$100—for the entire celebration of Christmas. If Christ walked into our community December 24th, I'm thinking that might be the home He'd prefer to visit.

Rx 16 *Enjoy Free Activities*

If we have the time to be creative and imaginative, many things in life can be enjoyed absolutely free. Borthwick gives the following suggestions:

- Catch up on the latest magazines at the local library
- Check out a video instead of renting one
- Read a book rather than shop
- Visit a free museum
- Take a bike ride
- Go sledding or skating
- Work on a hobby
- Exercise for free
- Play basketball at public courts or swim at a community pool
- Walk the stairs
- Barter child care or swap baby-sitting[15]

Often we might find these alternative options not only financially helpful but also healthier physically and relationally.

Rx 17 *Respect the Potential of Economic Volatility*
It is hard to write about economics today, because before the ink is dry the news is old. In this globalized world with electronic money flying at the speed of light, a hiccup in Asia can cause a seizure in Europe. More than one trillion dollars in foreign exchange routinely changes hands each day, far outstripping any central bank's ability to exercise control. A scandal in the Middle East can affect Wall Street—or vice versa. With the world fully wired and tightly coupled, volatility and vulnerability are everywhere. Don't get too ambitious leveraging the future with debt-sponsored schemes—they might sour before tomorrow morning's alarm clock goes off.

Rx 18 *Be Suspicious of Economic Answers*
Economics is entrenched as the most powerful force in Western society. The near universal advice we receive is that the economic road is the direction we should travel in order to solve our many problems. But God has an eternal feud with the power of money, and He begs to differ. The simple life is greatly facilitated if we agree with God on this matter. Money is perhaps the answer to some of life's problems. But the money solution is

never transcendent, and money is never the answer for the most important issues of the human condition.

Rx 19 *Use Debt as an Opportunity for Growth*
Mark Twain once quipped, "A person who has had a bull by the tail once has learned sixty to seventy times as much as a person who hasn't." As teachers, a bull and a debt have much in common. If debt has beaten us down, why not learn from the experience? If we will accept debt as being a valuable teacher of spiritual lessons, perhaps no better instructor exists.

Ask important and penetrating questions: Why did I get into debt in the first place? Am I controlled by my culture? Is my contentment linked to a consumerist lifestyle? Does my debt have spiritual implications? What would God have me learn through this process? If pain gets our attention, we should never waste the opportunity to grow.

Rx 20 *Change Your Measuring Stick*
Money is not the measure of all things. Perhaps it is time to remember "we live in a society, not an economy."[16] This same idea led economist E. F. Schumacher to write *Small Is Beautiful*, and to subtitle the book, *Economics as if People Mattered*. Before I had even opened the cover, I had learned from him.

Russ Crosson advises that we use a standard different from money for deciding our values. "Measure wealth not by the things you have, but by the things you have that you would not take money for."[17] If we could identify such a standard and integrate it practically into our everyday decision making, it would change most of our lives beyond recognition—*always* for the better.

CHAPTER 8

■ ■ ■ ■ ■ ■ ■ ■

Expectation

■ If you can dream it, you can do it. Now there's no limit to your ability.—PRUDENTIAL

■ Your world should know no boundaries.—MERRILL LYNCH

■ Life, liberty, and the pursuit of just about anything you please. Volvo—a car that can not only help save your life, but help save your soul.—VOLVO

■ We thought the way up is up. But with God, the way up is down.—WELLINGTON BOONE

A medical colleague bounded up to me, announcing,"I finally discovered the best way to get through the day. In the morning, I say to myself *This is going to be the worst day of my life.* Then when the day is only half horrible, I'm happy!" It was offered somewhat tongue-in-cheek, but along with the humor comes a good dose of wisdom: Our happiness and contentment are dependent on the expectations we bring to the experience. As progress gives us more and more benefits, it raises expectations. This, in turn, often makes it harder to find the happiness and contentment we seek.

One clear *advantage* of progress is that we have learned that life *can be* improved. But one clear *disadvantage* of progress is that we have come to expect that life *will be* improved. The expectation tends to rise faster than the improvement. Happiness versus unhappiness, satisfaction versus dissatisfaction, contentment versus discontentment are all contingent on expectation, not the actual improvement. If, for example, we expect one car and receive two, we are ecstatic. But if we expect three cars and receive two, we are crushed. In each case, we received two cars. The emotional result, however, was polar opposite.

Expectation overload is one of the most difficult to control. Our affluent, media-saturated age has spawned a rising tide of expectations. We expect health, wealth, and ease—and are discontent if more doesn't come, no matter how well-off we are. "The life of people on earth is obviously better now than it has ever been— certainly much better than it was 500 years ago when people beat each other with cats," reflects political observer Peggy Noonan. "This may sound silly but now and then when I read old fairy tales and see an illustration of a hunchbacked hag with no teeth and bumps on her nose who lives by herself in the forest, I think: People looked like that once. They lived like that. There were no doctors, no phones, and people lived in the dark in a hole in a tree. It was terrible. It's much better now. But we are not happier. I believe we are just cleaner, more attractive sad people than we used to be."[1]

GREAT EXPECTATIONS

Expectation overload. People everywhere are crumbling under the weight of it. In some ways, it is the most devastating of all overloads, driving the entire train of overload trauma. We are expected to be smart, or at least well educated; to be beautiful, fashionable, and athletic; to drive a nice car (without rust) and to live in a nice house (always picked up); to own nice things (at least as nice as the Joneses); to be the perfect parent and spouse. And lest we refuse to accept the terms and conditions of the first set of expectations, there is a final expectation standing guard over all the others: *We are expected to conform.* Let's examine some specifics.

Automobiles
The admission price to the good life expects that we drive a nice automobile—certainly befitting our career, income, and social status. One day when I worked my rotating shift at the Student Health Center in our university, my car was ticketed: "Please move your car. This spot is reserved for the physician." Why did the officer write

this note if not for an obvious cultural expectation that an M.D. would not drive a car like mine?

Homes
Over the past forty years, Americans have doubled the square footage in our homes even though families are smaller. Partly, as we will see, this is because of possession overload. But expectation overload is also to blame. Debt is not the determining factor in home size any-more — expectation is.

Fashion
Fashion has completely overwhelmed function — are we sure this is okay with God? If functionality were our only concern, most of us could survive on ten percent of our clothes budget. "Why exactly do we put on our 'Sunday best' to head out to church?" asks editorialist Doug Trouten. "The most common explanation is that we do it to honor God. Buried behind that explanation is the unspoken assumption that God is somehow going to feel honored because we're nicely dressed. But Isaiah tells us that to God 'our righteous acts are as filthy rags.' If that's how God feels about our righteousness, what makes us think He's going to like our suits?"[2]

Income
A dangerous expectation is that we need a lot of money to live on. Actually, the profound truth is that we need very little income to live a totally *God-honoring life.* Yes, perhaps we do need a huge cash flow to partake of the many benefits of our age. But people now struggling to make it on $100,000 could honor God completely with an income of $20,000. The rest is consumed purely in fulfillment of cultural expectation.

Careers
We expect our jobs to be stable, our careers to be faithful to us, our benefit packages to insulate us, and our company morale to meet our emotional needs. But in this era of downsizing, millions have been disappointed, displaced, and depressed by occupational insecurity and financial uncertainty.

Retirement

The expectation of retirement is a distinctly modern notion, historically speaking, and some predict it is transient. Indeed, they say, there is only a short window of time in only a few countries when such a luxury was possible at all. Yet we see people today who have retirement plans with millions of dollars who are nevertheless panicked that the money will not last. This is, of course, directly related to expectations.

Government

Big expectations have also encumbered big government in the form of rising entitlements: Social Security, Medicare, Medicaid, Welfare. Many social dilemmas have been appropriately addressed with these programs, and much societal suffering has been relieved. But, on the other hand, with each entitlement comes a commensurate expectation. And this expectation often traps people in dependency even as it traps government in untouchable budgetary spending.

Medicine

Expectations in medicine have risen to unattainable levels. We expect our doctor to know all the answers, our insurance to pay all the bills, and our body to heal all the ills. When these inappropriate expectations are not met, we look for someone to blame.

Plastic Surgery

Plastic surgery is yet another manifestation of our overblown expectations. Many, upset at nature for not giving them a perfect body, spend enormous sums attempting to buy one. If we didn't care how we (or others) looked on the outside, concentrating instead on the inner qualities of integrity, virtue, and purity, perhaps we would mature beyond our fixation with looks.

In Argentina, people openly boast of recent plastic surgeries, showing off their bandages and bruises around the eyes, and ask each other on television "Where did you have your nose job?" The president of the country flaunts his six plastic surgeries. I don't want to stigmatize it, but do we really wish to normalize it?

Mental Health
One modern expectation was that progress would solve our mental and emotional suffering through the benefits of education, wealth, technology, health care, and convenience. Such has not been the case. This profound disappointment has, in turn, made our depression and anxiety even more painful.

Education
Society expects us to get an education. And holding a degree, we expect that life will magically unfold. But, of course, many college students don't have a clue what to study, can't get a job in their field, and are surprised when an education does not prepare them for such all important real-life events as relationships, emotional well-being, and spiritual fulfillment.

Sports
Professional players get multi-million dollar contracts but seem less happy and more self-absorbed than ever. One recent NBA player, two years out of high school, turned down $17 million a year. While I don't completely condemn players for exploring fair market value, it is perverse to assume that happiness and contentment will come along with the expected top dollar.

Marriage
Our modern expectations of marriage are, at the same time, very low and very high. On the one hand, expectations are low in that we anticipate trouble. Even on the way to the altar, some are already wondering if the marriage can last. On the other hand, expectations are high in the sense that we place on our mate extraordinary demands to make us happy and meet our needs. In short, we demand more and put up with less.

Parenting
Parental expectations for our children often crush the child out of them. "The concept of childhood, so vital to the traditional American way of life, is threatened with extinction in the society we have created," writes child psychologist David Elkind. "Today's child has

become the unwilling, unintended victim of overwhelming stress—
the stress borne of rapid, bewildering social change and constantly
rising expectations."[3] We begin hurrying them in education when
they are still in the cradle, we want them to be beauty queens or football stars when they are six, and we insist on straight A's when they
hit junior high. Whatever happened to unconditional love?

Traditions and Rituals

Why are modern weddings and funerals so outrageously expensive?
Because the expectation bar has been raised impossibly high and no
one has the fortitude to resist the flow. To be a good fiancé, one must
show his love by purchasing the biggest diamond. To be loving parents, we must offer the most expensive wedding. To be good children, we must purchase a "respectable" casket. To be doting
grandparents, we must flood the grandchildren with Christmas toys.

ADS, THE MEDIA, COMMERCIALIZATION, AND THE LAW

This extraordinary level of expectation derives from many different
cultural forces, but chief among them are advertisements, the media,
the commercialization of everyday life, and the legal system.

Everywhere we go, ads stare us down and draw us in. It is hard
to avoid them, and as a matter of fact, we often are not even fully
aware of their presence. Teenagers, on average, are exposed to
360,000 advertisements before they graduate from high school.[4]
David Wolfe, creative director of a consulting firm, believes the
communications explosion has "made it possible for everybody,
even in the armpit of the outback, to know what cool is."[5] Movies
are increasingly hawking products within the context of the plot.

Children, who daily watch up to five hours of television,
including one hour of commercials, represent a manipulatable
and recession-proof market. When confronted with Avon's line of
Barbie cosmetics, critic Alex Molnar asked, "What's next, pre-
natal lipstick?"[6] One toiletry manufacturer is marketing solid
deodorant for seven-year-olds—even though such children have
no physiological need for the product until at least age eleven.

Additionally, products for children are increasingly sold on the basis of rebellion. "Just watch a Saturday morning's worth of TV commercials, and see how many products are sold by making the appeal that your parents won't like you to have this product," observes Kenneth Myers.[7] Yet the rebellion themes don't stop with children. Modern advertising is not only causing inordinate expectations but also driving the deeper problem of societal discord. Joseph Turow, a professor of communications, has discovered a "revolutionary shift" in the strategies and tactics of marketing companies, which, he says, "has been driven by, and has been driving, a profound sense of division in American society." Turow believes that advertisers, working in concert with conglomerating media companies, are forcing "a breakdown in social cohesion" in the United States.[8]

"Advertisers are focusing more and more on the emerging market of 'people who do only what they want to do,'" observes columnist John Leo, "that is, people who yearn to be completely free of all restraint, expectations, and responsibilities." Burger King offers, *Sometimes, you gotta break the rules.* A shoe company promises their shoe *conforms to your foot so you don't have to conform to anything.* Says Nike, *We are all hedonists and we want what feels good. That's what makes us human.* "The point here," explains Leo, "is that while everyone is aghast over blatant sex, violent movies, and gangsta rap, the ordinary commercial messages of corporate America are probably playing a more subversive role."[9]

No small contributor to the expectation problem, the legal profession must accept considerable blame. "There is some form of mass neurosis that leads many people to think courts were created to solve all the problems of mankind," accused former Chief Justice of the Supreme Court Warren Burger, saying many lawsuits are "an exercise in futility" best solved by other means.[10] Our national "victimization" epidemic is directly related to expectations exploited by the legal profession.

PRESCRIPTIONS FOR CORRECTING OUR EXPECTATION INFLATION

In light of ever-increasing societal expectations, what can we do to counteract these pressures? Many of the possible adjustments have to do with our mindset and lifestyle.

Rx 1 *Respect Limits*

We must realize our limits and become comfortable accepting them. We can't be superpastor, superteacher, or superparent all the time, and neither should we try. As a physician, I can't memorize all three thousand pages of the *Physician's Desk Reference*. Even Jesus didn't heal every disease in Israel.

Some have said, "Your God is too small." I agree! But I would also add, "We are too large." When we inflate our role in the drama of life and increase our own personal expectations beyond the realm of human possibility, we crash and burn against the Almighty's intentions. Remember, limits were His idea.

Rx 2 *Adjust Your Expectations*

"Expect more and you'll get it," says the MasterCard ad. Implicit in the message is that it is always *appropriate* to expect more. But as we adjust our expectations downward, we will discover less to be unhappy about.

If we always expect success and prosperity, we are destined to be chronically frustrated. But if we understand that humankind is fallen and life is difficult, we are more likely to be contented with the simple blessings God sends our way.

Rx 3 *Redefine Enough*

Perhaps the best way to deal with the expectation of always having enough is to diminish our definition of that word. For most of us, according to Vicki Robin, *enough* is *"more* than we have now." But if we instead defined *enough* as *"what* we have now," our expectations will be fulfilled. "It's the old idea that the less you want, the richer you are," says physician and marathoner George Sheehan, explaining the secret of his long career. "I try to make my life free of wants and restrict it to needs."[11]

Rx 4 *Compare Yourself to the Less Fortunate*

Expectations expand when we look at cars nicer than ours and friends who have swimming pools. Our well-being is sabotaged by envying movie stars with beauty and bodies to match. So, instead, let's look elsewhere. "After days of traveling in East

Africa, I was numb from witnessing the poverty," writes simplicity author David A. Sorensen. "'Are these people happy?' I asked John, our Masai guide. 'They have much happiness here,' he replied. 'It all depends on what you compare your own lifestyle with, don't you think?'"[12] If they are happy in their destitution, and we are unhappy in our affluence, perhaps we have some recalibration to do.

Rx 5 *Beware the Trap of Winning*

Success begets increased expectations. "We not only have successes, we become our successes," explains Henri Nouwen. "And the more we allow our accomplishments . . . to become the criteria of our self-esteem, the more we are . . . never sure if we will be able to live up to the expectations which we created by our last successes. In many people's lives, there is a nearly diabolic chain in which their anxieties grow according to their successes."[13]

"People can become psychologically trapped by their own success as they race to keep up with the rising expectations bred by each new achievement," observes psychologist Gilbert Brim. "With each success they raise their level of difficulty, climbing up a ladder of subgoals, moving faster, raising aspirations and at some point reaching the limit of their capacity.

"At this point, successful performance becomes difficult and people begin to lose more often than they win. Their resources are squeezed to the utmost. The business executive, promoted beyond a level of just manageable difficulty, ends up being held together by a thin paste of alcohol, saunas, and antibiotics."[14]

Let the "winner" beware. Even as you set high standards and pursue lofty goals, always keep one eye on the threshold of your limits. Once success catapults you into the world of overload, the rules of the game change. It is wise to make adjustments commensurate with the amount of overloading.

Rx 6 *Tune Out Ads*

As we have seen, expectation inflation often comes from advertisements. Since most ads are nothing more than avenues of discontent through "need creation," wage war against them. Perhaps the most powerful way to accomplish this is to control the television. After twenty years of an old, black-and-white television, we finally purchased a color set because the remote control shifts the balance of power back into our hands as parents. When ads come on, we use the remote to switch the channel. Even though our children dislike this annoying habit, it accomplishes two things: It keeps us from seeing and absorbing the content of the ads, and it teaches our kids that we are serious about the false content of advertisements.

Rx 7 *De-emphasize Respectability in Fashion*

How often we change cars, wardrobes, furniture, and carpeting because of the burdensome assumptions about the opinions of others. Don't change fashion because someone else thinks it should be done. We are capable of judging function without the prejudicial expectations of others clouding our thinking.

Wearing only middle-of-the-road clothes, I virtually never make a fashion statement. But I have found great contentment in fashion mediocrity. Our fashion expectations are easier to fulfill when we buy things for usefulness rather than status.

Rx 8 *Simplify Holidays, Ceremonies, and Rituals*

In Pittsburgh, writes Chuck Colson, "all holidays from Thanksgiving through Christmas and New Year's have been blended into a gargantuan commercial celebration called *Sparkle Season.*"[15] I am not a scrooge, but my advice is this: Forget about Sparkle Season and all the obligatory trappings. Get back to the basics in ceremonies and celebrations: family, faith, friends. Some suggestions:

Christmas: Reduce the money expenditures. Simplify, simplify. Cut expectations to only those Christ Himself would endorse.

Engagements: Instead of a diamond for engagement, Linda and I decided on the Swedish custom of two gold bands—one for the engagement and one for the wedding. We still endorse the idea twenty-seven happily married years later.

Weddings: One wedding in Boston was held in a garden where, instead of gifts, the bride and groom requested that people bring food for the reception dinner. Friends provided the music, served the meal, and took the photographs. Total cost? Chair rental.

Funerals: When my brother-in-law died prematurely at the age of fifty, his two sons built him a pine casket. It was wonderfully respectful, and all I would ever want myself.

Rx 9 *Resist Inflated Housing Expectations*

Just because we have the ability to buy an expensive home seems to convey a commensurate expectation that we will do exactly that. When a real estate agent handed Barbara and David Sorensen the keys to a downsized, 950 square-foot house, he said, "But I still don't get it. Why'd you buy such a small house, anyway?" Buying beneath one's ability seemed unusual to him. The Sorensens explained their desire for a simpler life, one more consistent with their values.

When the realtor described the extravagant house he was building, the Sorensens asked, "Why are you building such a big house?" He looked startled, not used to being challenged about such an obvious thing. "Well, because I can!" he replied.[16] If you want financial margin for decades to come, resist the expectation to buy bigger than you need.

Rx 10 *Free Others*

When we put too many expectations on others, they return the favor. In this hypercritical, grace-devoid, expectation-overloaded world, we need to set one another free. When we expect too much of others, we suffocate them. And when they do not fulfill our unreasonable demands, we frustrate ourselves. "Never, never pin your whole faith on any human being: not if he is the best and wisest in the whole world," advises C. S. Lewis. "There are lots of nice things you can do with sand; but do not try building a house on it."[17]

Rx 11 *Give Your Pastor a Break*

The pastorate has gone from a "low stress, high reward" job to a "high stress, low reward" job. Never was a job created with more conflicting expectations. Pastor's families are expected to be perfect, with spouses who have exceptional ministry gifts and children who are the most godly and best behaved. In addition, we expect modern churches to have endless programs for our ever-expanding needs. But of course, no one has time to volunteer—so guess who gets the job?

"Pastors can carry heavy loads, but there's a point at which it becomes too much," warns psychiatrist Louis McBurney, M.D. "Needs of the congregation combine with the pastor's own need to be needed, pushing the load beyond the breaking point."[18] If we want healthy, invested pastors, let's hire wisely and then set them free. Totally.

Rx 12 *Free Your Spouse*
Freedom is a key to any successful marriage. Not the narcissistic kind, the grace kind. As we relinquish control and lower expectations, the marital bond surprisingly solidifies. "If there is any area in our relationships as couples that controls our ability to gain inner rest, I believe it is the expectations we bring to our marriage," explains author Tim Kimmel. "As I counsel couples getting married—and couples trying to stay married—this is the one area I emphasize beyond all others. . . . What I need to do is come to a relationship with expectations that only cover *me*. After all, I'm the only person over whom I have control."[19]

Rx 13 *Love Unconditionally*
Give children a chance to grow up naturally, slowly, innocently. They should have paper dolls and earthworms at age six, not Latin tests and figure-skating competitions. The best way for making the entire parenting experience positive and peaceful is to give age-appropriate expectations, delivered with unconditional love.

Rx 14 *Don't Serve on a Silver Platter*
I fear for the future of today's children who have everything handed them on a silver platter. Many parents feel their children should experience all the benefits that progress has to offer. But I view the silver platter as a liability that greatly increases their expectation level in an uncertain future.

"For any happiness, even in this world, quite a lot of restraint is going to be necessary," explains C. S. Lewis.[20] That restraining process should gently begin at the hands of wise parents, who carefully hide the silver platter under the dish towel. But instead, warns sociologist Arlie Hochschild, overworked parents often overindulge their children out of guilt from absentee parenting.[21]

If you wish to invest in your child's future, don't raise their materialistic appetites and expectations. Instead, teach them the enormous secret found in biblical contentment.[22]

Rx 15 *Free Yourself from the Opinion of Others*

Perhaps the biggest burden we carry is our inordinate concern about the opinion of others. If we could free ourselves from that weighty expectation, we would find ourselves on freedom's road.

"The heart's fierce effort to protect itself from every slight, to shield its touchy honor from the bad opinion of friend and enemy, will never let the mind have rest. Continue this fight through the years and the burden will become intolerable," explains theologian A. W. Tozer. "Such a burden as this is not necessary to bear. Jesus calls us to His rest, and meekness is His method. The meek man cares not at all who is greater than he, for he has long ago decided that the esteem of the world is not worth the effort."[23]

Rx 16 *Deny Yourself*

If we want an expectation correction, try Christ. "If anyone would come after me," Jesus preached, "he must deny himself and take up his cross and follow me."[24] Denying ourselves is a normal and expected part of the Christian life. It is akin to fasting with this difference: Fasting is episodic; self-denial is lifelong. Christ did it for us. We do it for Him.

Yet, practically speaking, what do we deny ourselves? For many of us, the answer is virtually nothing. The requirement of self-denial is not for punishing us, but rather for focusing us and freeing us. It clears our head of the world and its many expectations, and points us in the direction of things that matter most.

CHAPTER 9

■ ■ ■ ■ ■ ■ ■ ■

Hurry and Fatigue

■ Man is flying too fast for a world that is round. Soon he will catch up with himself in a great rear end collision, and man will never know that what hit him from behind was man.—JAMES THURBER

■ Drowsy drivers may kill as many people as drunken drivers.—BERKELEY WELLNESS LETTER

■ Fatigue makes cowards of us all.—VINCE LOMBARDI

■ I learned to tell time and now I'm always late.
—LILLY TOMLIN AS EDITH ANN

The world seems to have an automatically advancing speed rheostat, and every year the treadmill spins faster. American culture, reports editorialist Mortimer B. Zuckerman, "is strapped to a rocket whose velocity and range we can only faintly comprehend."[1]

"America. The land of the rushed," complains small town journalist Peg Zaemisch. "We have proudly defined our American lifestyle as 'life in the fast lane.' Now, we rush to construct passing lanes, so we can get around those pokie-schmokies in the fast lane . . . do they think we've got all day? We've become a country of out-of-breath-red-faced folks, racing around with our hair permanently blowing back." Zaemisch vows to tame her "catch-a-bullet-in-my-teeth schedule—just as soon as I get off this deadline."[2]

Even our sentences are peppered with such words as *time crunch, fast food, rush hour, frequent flyer, expressway, overnight delivery,* and *rapid transit.* The products and services we use further attest to our hurry: We send packages by Federal Express, use a long distance company called Sprint, manage our personal finances on

Quicken, schedule our appointments on a DayRunner, diet with SlimFast, and swim in trunks made by Speedo. "The society in which we live today would have us believe, or at least hope, that life will be okay if we can just get it packaged right and served to us on the run," observes publisher Bob Benson.[3]

In Montana, where speed limits are "reasonable and prudent," a man was clocked going 150 miles per hour. In the Nevada desert, a British speed burner set a new land speed record by going 764.168 miles per hour—breaking the sound barrier for the first time in a land-based vehicle. Elsewhere, an impatient Purdue engineer, frustrated with how long it took charcoal briquettes to light, decided to pipe in pure oxygen. It worked so well, he decided to use liquid oxygen—the kind used in booster rockets. That worked well too—he burned up all the briquettes and the grill in three seconds. "It was pretty bright," he said. "You didn't want to look at it."

BREAKING LIFE'S SPEED LIMIT

An eighty-nine-year-old man watched with dismay as his physician rushed breathlessly from room to room, patient to patient. Finally he reached out and grabbed the doctor by the arm. "Doc," he said, "you're goin' so fast you're passin' up more stuff than you're catchin' up to."

Although physicians know the syndrome well, our profession isn't alone in being plagued by this hurry sickness—the entire world seems caught up in it. Of course we all enjoy going fast, at least from time to time. But the enormous increase in the speed of daily life is clearly pathogenic. We live in a nanosecond culture, wheezing and worn-out.

Speed. Hurry. We pay a price for the pace at which we live. The late French historian Jacques Ellul commented, "No one knows where we are going, the aim of life has been forgotten, the end has been left behind. Man has set out at tremendous speed—to go *nowhere*."[4]

"These days, speed is of the essence," observes David Sharp of *USA Today*. "Anything that can't keep up becomes the cultural equivalent of roadkill."[5] Yes, the world is going faster. And yes, we in turn are also going faster. But the important question no one asks is this: When does *faster* become *too fast?*

Is there a speed limit to life? What happens when we exceed it? Does God give us a ticket? I have thought long and hard about the issue of speed and have come to believe that it is as much responsible for the problem of personal and societal dysfunction as any other single factor.

Virtually all of our relationships are damaged by hurry. Many families are being starved to death by velocity. Our children lie wounded on the ground, run over by our high-speed good intentions.

Why do we hurry our kids? Mostly, because *we* are in a hurry. "Parents were asked to go to the auditorium to hear the school band play some Mozart before we met the teachers," explained Elizabeth Berg about attending a school conference. "The musical director was careful to point out that the piece would take only two minutes. I looked at the expectant kids seated behind him, waiting to entertain us with their very best. The director said what he did because he could see us tight-lipped parents looking at our watches. I was deeply ashamed, and I thought, *If we don't have time for children playing Mozart, what do we have time for?*"[6]

God, I suspect, doesn't fit any better into our breakneck schedules than our children do. We walk fast, talk fast, eat fast, and then announce, "Sorry, I've got to run." The trouble is, God's not running after us. He knows that speed does not yield devotion. He knows that with all our running we're just opening an ever greater distance between where we're running to and where He's waiting for us. I think I would not be far wrong if I were to postulate that our sense of the presence of God is in inverse proportion to the pace of our lives.

Have you ever noticed that Jesus never seemed to be in a hurry? The Bible never says anything about Him running. Apparently, Jesus believed that very little of lasting spiritual or emotional value happens in the presence of speed. Jesus understood that busyness, productivity, and efficiency are speed words, not kingdom words. At times they are appropriate values—but they are never transcendent. Jesus understood that meditation, wisdom, and worship are slow, mellow, and deep.

FATIGUE OVERLOAD

When speed and busyness have matured, they give birth to fatigue. Americans are, if anything, exhausted. We are a nation of the *hard-wired and dog-tired*. Seminary president and author Chuck Swindoll claims our era is "the age of the half-read page, the quick hash and the mad dash, the bright night with the nerves tight, the plane hop with the brief stop, the lamp tan in a short span, the brain strain and the heart pain, the catnaps until the spring snaps . . . the land where the fun's gone."[7]

Fatigue, I should quickly point out, is a normal occurrence. It happens to all people and at all points in history. But that doesn't mean that all fatigue is equal. In many ways, today's "universal fatigue," as Swiss psychiatrist Paul Tournier called it, is a surprise. Progress, it was reasonable to expect, should lead to restedness and leisure. That we should have such weariness in body and spirit was not predicted.

Fatigue, of course, comes from many sources for many reasons. But contributing greatly to our current epidemic is our frenzied AWOL—"American Way of Life." In the context of this chapter, three common sources of fatigue—sleep deprivation, deconditioning, and stress—deserve special mention. Each is directly related to progress, overload, busyness, and hurry.

Fatigue from Sleep Deprivation

It is perhaps true that modern Americans get less sleep than at any other time in history. In 1850, for example, the average American got 9.5 hours of sleep per night. By 1950, that had decreased to 8 hours. Currently, it is 7 hours—and still declining. As a result, fifty to seventy million Americans (depending on which study you read) have sleep disorders.

Why, under the tutelage of progress, have the hours of sleep declined so dramatically? The answer is simple: electricity and the light bulb. We are now a twenty-four-hour-a-day society that seldom shuts down.

Fatigue from Deconditioning

Deconditioning is a second major cause of our fatigue problem, again, compliments of modernity. Once progress delivered us from the need to use our muscles in earning a living, we lost both strength and stamina. Now, we must artificiate ways to get the exercise we need. But who likes to sweat? Who likes the pain? And who has the time anyway?

Fatigue from Stress

There is no clinical doubt but that the mind writes prescriptions for the body and the body obediently complies. The greater the stress, the greater the feelings of tiredness, exhaustion, and burnout. While these feelings of fatigue are real, there is nothing for your physician to measure. The best antidote for this type of fatigue is a program of stress management combined with wise stress reduction.

PRESCRIPTIONS FOR HEALING THE HURRY SICKNESS

As the world around us accelerates, our energies wane. But we are not defenseless victims. The following suggestions will help replace frenzy with peace and rest.

Rx 1 *Consciously Slow the Pace of Life*

I recently saw a T-shirt that read: "It's not the pace of life that worries me. It's the sudden stop at the end." After contemplation, I decided the exact opposite is true. "The sudden stop at the end" means a home-going that, quite frankly, I look forward to. But *the pace of life is deadly!*

Is it possible to consciously slow our pace? Of course it is. We just have to say *no* more often. It is not easy, but it is necessary— and it is right.

Every year the world spins faster. So put on the brakes and obey the speed limit of your soul. The green pastures and still waters yet await us—but not in the direction the treadmill is spinning.[8]

As the "Old Negro Ballad" pleads:

Slo' me down, Lord
I'm movin' too fast.
Don't know my own brother
When he's awalkin' past.
Miss the best things o' life
Day by day.

Don't know a blessin'
When it comes my way.

Rx 2 *Make Technology Work For You and Not Against You*

Remember: Time-saving technologies don't save time. Instead, they compress and consume time. Recognizing that technology is responsible for much of our time urgency problem, it is appropriate to be skeptical. Clocks, watches, alarms, computers, answering machines, cell phones, pagers, and fax machines often create more time problems than they solve. Use them judiciously.

Always make technology work *for you* and not *against you.* If you can't control it, don't trust it. "The high-tech world of clocks and schedules, computers and programs, was supposed to free us from a life of toil and deprivation," explains technology critic Jeremy Rifkin in *Time Wars,* "yet with each passing day the human race becomes more . . . exploited and victimized."[9]

Leaving a workshop where I had just spoken, a dentist took off his watch and flipped it into the swimming pool. You might not wish to be quite this dramatic. But, then again. . . .

Rx 3 *Throw Away the Alarm Clock*

Psychiatrist Paul Meier provocatively asserts, "If you wake up to an alarm every morning, there is a good chance that you are out of the will of God." Radical thinking! But he is simply trying to shock us into rethinking the will of God in light of the original equipment provided at Creation. An alarm clock was not a part of the package. Instead, God caused our bodies to generally wake up when we had enough sleep. Now, however, that natural process never gets a chance to complete itself.

Rx 4 *Repent of the Pride of Busyness*

The busier we appear, the greater the respect afforded us. While the person sitting on a lawn swing is scorned, the speed-of-light jet jockey is venerated.

"The clock dictates the tempo of our lives," explains Mayo Gilson, M.D. "We all hurry, involving others in our hurry. Paradoxically, we point to our lack of time with a certain pride, as if that lack has something to do with our importance as a person."[10] There is a trap here, and pride is its name. Before we can slow down and allow God to set things right in our hearts, we have some confessing to do. It is not busyness that we should honor in our midst, but love. Busyness and love are not the same. One is speed; the other is God.

Rx 5 *"Ruthlessly Eliminate Hurry"*

When John Ortberg moved from California to Illinois to assume a position at the rapidly growing Willow Creek Community Church, he first asked a wise mentor for advice. "You must ruthlessly eliminate hurry from your life," said his friend. Ortberg wrote down the advice and then waited for the next suggestion. "There is nothing else," explained the sage.[11]

I am struck by three aspects of this truth: how *simple* it is, how *difficult* it is, and how *ruthless* it is. *Ruthless* is indeed the best word to use in this context, because no other degree of intention is sufficient to accomplish such a goal.

Rx 6 *Take Your Time*

Persistence, the tortoise taught the hare, is more important than speed. Life is a marathon, not a sprint. The person who sprints wins the hundred-yard-dash—but loses the marathon. Business executive John Capozzi, in his best-selling collection of favorite maxims, illustrates the principle well:

■ The race is not always won by the fastest runner but sometimes by those who just keep running.
■ Measure twice . . . cut once.
■ Avoid shortcuts. They always take too much time in the long run.
■ To finish sooner, take your time.[12]

Rx 7 *Set an Earlier ETA*

Moderns do not like to arrive early and barely agree to arrive on time. We plan our schedules so that we can arrive "somewhere in the vicinity"—meaning give or take ten minutes. But then when traffic is snarled, or unexpected snow falls, or we get a late start, or the car is out of gas, we begin to hurry. And worry. The entire experience quickly erodes into yet another urgency-induced panic attack.

To short-circuit such routine disasters, plan to arrive early. With an earlier ETA (estimated time of arrival), you can slow down the driving, enjoy the day, and actually begin to anticipate with pleasure the event in front of you. The best way to accomplish an ETA, of course, is to have an earlier ETD (estimated time of departure).

Rx 8 *Turn Back the Clock*

Occasionally live one day in 1930, 1900, or 1850. You might be surprised at how delightful—and slow-paced—such an adventure turns out to be. When you commit to such an experience, use only the technology that existed during that era. This rule, of course, never precludes walking, reading, talking, or sleeping.

By eliminating our modern hurrying technologies—even for a day—it will quickly become apparent just how large a role these devices play in the unreasonable pace of life.

Rx 9 *Understand the Difference between Time and Time*

As it turns out, not all time is created equal. According to pastor Arthur Dunn, the Bible distinguishes between *kairos* and *chronos*. Kairos is *significant time*: meaningful, vertical, quality time—where Jesus lived. Chronos is *clock time*: linear, simple, chronological, measurable, quantity time—where we live.

While *chronos* is occupied with the linear measurement of the past, present, and future, *kairos* is occupied with nonlinear measurements that are event-conscious, life-focused, and meaning-sensitive. Busyness and productivity are usually activities of *chronos,* while spirituality and relationships are usually activities of *kairos.*

"Do people need help managing time because they are too busy?" asks Dunn. "Or do they need help managing time because they have lost the sense of the meaning of time?"[13] "The Bible calls us to live first by kairos [significant time]," explains author Ben Patterson, "and to let kairos dictate to chronos [clock time] what we will do and how we will live."[14]

I am convinced that if we understood this fundamental truth, both our hurry and our fatigue would disappear in the same holy breeze.

Rx 10 *Develop Healthy Sleep Habits*

Progress gave us the light bulb; the light bulb invaded the night; and sleep never recovered from the shock. Sleep was God's idea, and good sleep is restorative. Value sleep. *Choose* to get enough sleep. To be well-rested is a blessing, not a waste of time. Learn to enjoy a nap without feeling guilty.

Buy a good mattress—you will spend a third of your life there. I don't even mind if your mattress costs more than your car. Don't have disturbing conversations immediately before bedtime. Like the time Linda said to me, "Better get a good night's sleep, because there's something we need to talk about in the morning."

Rx 11 *Develop an Exercise Program*

In the first instance, progress took away exercise through technology and the subsequent automation of our lives. In the second instance, progress keeps exercise away through hurry and fatigue. But if given a chance, exercise works well to counteract fatigue overload.

Perhaps because exercise isn't our favorite activity, many of us conveniently never find time for it. But if we include it in a balanced budget of time usage, exercise will often reimburse us minute for minute. The increased vitality resulting from good conditioning allows more energy and efficiency for all other endeavors.

Rx 12 *Schedule Relational Time*

In our speed-driven lifestyles, relational health will not happen unless we intentionally make it happen. Hurry and intimacy are two entirely different things. Let's slow down so that our family and friends can be included in our schedules. "What they'll remember most about their childhood when they grow older are two things," explains educational consultant Buck Sterling. "How much love was in the home, and how much time you spent with them."[15]

Bob Benson came home late one night, but still made the rounds kissing his children in bed—a nightly routine. "I bent over and kissed Patrick on the cheek and quickly stood up and started out of the room. . . . His question stopped me cold and brought me back to his bedside. 'Why do you kiss me so fast?'"[16]

Begrudge not love its time.

Rx 13 *Schedule Margin Time*

"I believe that one of the supreme aims of a man's life should be to secure a margin," wrote Australian F. W. Boreham in 1915. "A good life, like a good book, should have a good margin. . . . The most winsome people in the world are the people who make you feel that they are never in a hurry."[17]

As we have seen, Jesus never seemed in a hurry. Time urgency was not only absent from His life, it was conspicuously absent. Creating a margin—that space between our load and our limits—is perhaps one of the best ways to allow Christlike spontaneity and interruptibility back into our lives. Margin blunts hurry and allows us to focus on the divine appointments God sends our way.

Margin tames hurry as few other forces can. But it works both ways. Hurry can also make short work of margin.

Rx 14 *Understand the Will of God*

Clearly understanding the will of God will solve both our hurry and fatigue overload in the same revelation. God is not so desperate for resources or power that He must assign us twice as big a load as we can possibly carry. Certainly, He will at times place extraordinary demands upon us. But this is for the purpose of refining us, not because His external objective is otherwise beyond His reach.

"We can be quite sure that whatever God wishes us to devote ourselves to He will grant us time enough in which to do it," explains Robert Banks. "Our responsibility is to find out exactly what He wants and hold resolutely to that. One of our greatest problems is that we misunderstand what God asks of us, either by adding all kinds of extra responsibilities or by possessing only a hazy idea of what He wishes. We will gain more time by properly understanding His will for us than by all the time-saving suggestions put together."[18]

Rx 15 *Wait*

Waiting on God has been a mainstay of theology for three millennia. Yet over the last thirty years, we have sacrificed this important truth and don't even have the wisdom to realize it's been a serious loss. If we are fatigued, exhausted, and hurrying to and fro with no rest in sight, is it possible that "waiting upon the Lord" is the answer to our problem? "They that wait upon the Lord shall renew their strength."[19]

"I found myself hurrying God," says author and pastor Henry Blackaby. "I just kind of fit Him in wherever He needed to be fit in. And one day God said to me, 'Henry, you're not going to hurry me any more. I'm not going to fit around your schedule — you're going to fit around mine.' That changed my whole life."[20]

If we will not recover the discipline of waiting, God is under no moral obligation to speed up His timetable to accommodate our urgency.

"Rest in the LORD and wait patiently for Him. . . ."[21]

CHAPTER 10

■ ■ ■ ■ ■ ■ ■ ■

Information and Education

- If the most conscientious physician were to attempt to keep up with the literature by reading two articles per day, in one year this individual would be more than eight hundred years behind.—OCTO BARNETT, M.D.

- The Library of Congress contains more than 100 million documents housed on 650 miles of shelving.

- We're all overloaded. We're sending E-mail to somebody fifty feet away.—DIANE SCHWARZ, FINANCIAL SYSTEMS MANAGER

- [Information overload] is wild. It's killing people. In my office, I have fifteen televisions. I can't handle it all.—TED TURNER, DESCRIBED AS THE NATION'S NO. 1 NEWS JUNKIE

Drowning in data is now an expected everyday part of corporate life, where having too much information is as dangerous as having too little. Information glut is causing off-the-chart stress levels and growing job dissatisfaction. "The synergistic evolution of computer and telecommunications technologies," explains journalist William Auckerman, "has created a world in which the quantity of information reaching our desks is growing exponentially, far surpassing the linear ability of the human brain to assimilate and process it."[1] Chalk up yet another casualty at the hands of progress.

"Unless we can discover ways of staying afloat amidst the surging torrents of information," warns psychologist Dr. David Lewis, "we may end up drowning in them."[2] The 1996 Reuter's study "Dying for Information" details the increasingly common symptoms of the *Information Fatigue Syndrome*: anxiety, self-doubt, paralysis of analytical capacity, a tendency to blame others, time-wasting, and in some cases illness.

Even though the respondents to this international survey of

managers claim they require high levels of information to do their jobs efficiently, forty-one percent said their working environments are extremely stressful on a daily basis, sixty-one percent report that their personal relationships have suffered, and ninety-four percent do not believe the situation will improve.

Rush Hour on the Information Superhighway

There are some who believe the rapidly emerging information super-highway will solve our problems. I don't. If our diagnosis were *too little information coming too slowly,* then the information super-highway would obviously help. But that is not our diagnosis. In fact, we already have too much information coming too fast. How do you put out a fire with gasoline?

As we have seen repeatedly, there are only so many details in anyone's life that can be handled comfortably. When that limit is exceeded, circuits begin to shut down. We refuse to process any more. Yet progress has given us more information in the past thirty years than in all the previous *five thousand years combined.*[3]

Francis Bacon, a contemporary of Shakespeare, is regarded by historians as the last person to know everything in the world. Since then, each of us learns a progressively smaller percentage of all the information that exists. As you might expect, with the explosive growth in information, the gap grows exponentially wider.

Furthermore, there is no reason to suspect that the situation will suddenly reverse, giving us a chance to catch up. Of all the scientists who have ever lived, ninety percent are alive today—each creating, processing, and distributing information. The doubling time of scientific knowledge is remarkably short. The rate at which information is discovered and disseminated exceeds—by many orders of magnitude—our limited ability to learn.

During residency orientation, I tell the young doctors that despite working eighty hours a week for three years doing nothing but learning, they will graduate from residency further behind than when they came. It is frustrating to work that hard, yet slip backward. But I also quickly tell them not to worry—most information exists in the form of pollution, of absolutely no use to them or their patients.

THE PERISHABILITY OF FACT

A surprising and discomforting aspect of this incredible information proliferation is that the more we know, the more certainty seems to recede. We had expected that with the progressive evolution of knowledge, we would hone in on a truth and finally nail it down. The opposite has happened.

Instead of becoming more certain about the truth, we become more insecure. I no longer believe there is a single right answer to a patient's problem. There is only *today's answer.* Don't misunderstand—I am not a therapeutic nihilist. Just a realist who has been around too long and outlived my informational innocence. The half-life of fact is not very long these days. Alfred North Whitehead observed: "Knowledge does not keep any better than fish."[4]

Physicians aren't fond of this development, even less, our patients. But, of course, such dislike doesn't change the universe's opinion of things. Nobody much likes the uncertainty principle, but that doesn't mean we get to repeal it. "Doctors are uncomfortable with uncertainty," explains psychiatrist Paul Fink, M.D. "In fact, our entire system of medical education is constructed as if everything were certain. The fact that what is certain today will be obsolete tomorrow has little influence upon faculties, students, and curriculum committees."[5] "Fifty percent of all we taught you is wrong," announced the President of Harvard Medical School at commencement. "The trouble is, we don't know which fifty percent."

Science is, after all, only "an orderly arrangement of what seem at the time to be facts."

DATACIDE

Everywhere you look, we are surrounded by data. The burgeoning amount of information available has strained all systems attempting to deal with it. A landmark edition of *The New York Times* (13 November 1987) was more than sixteen hundred pages long, contained more than two million lines of type comprised of twelve million words, and weighed twelve pounds. In Germany, the annual Frankfurt Book Fair is the world's largest, where seven thousand publishers from eighty countries show each other 350,000 titles.

According to David Shenk, author of *Data Smog,* paper consumption per capita in the United States tripled between 1940 and 1980, and tripled again between 1980 and 1990. In the average office, sixty percent of each person's time is spent processing documents. The typical business manager is said to read one million words per week.[6]

In one year, 230 journals, 3,200 journal articles, and 50,000 pages of material came across my desk. All of which were, of course, dutifully squirreled away for that illusory day when I will have the time to read them—especially that *New England Journal's* lead article, "Genetic Linkage of the Marfan Syndrome, Ectopia Lentis, and Congenital Contractural Arachnodactyly to the Fibrillin Genes on Chromosomes 15 and 5."

Using transistors etched onto microchips, computerization has thrown the information age into turbo gear. Every month, four quadrillion transistors are produced—*more than half a million for every human on the planet* and each costing far less than a staple. More than seven million transistors are etched on each tiny Pentium II chip, in lines one four-hundredth the thickness of a human hair.[7] It is now possible to cram 11.6 gigabytes of data into one square inch of disk space, which is equivalent to storing an eighteen-story stack of double-spaced typed pages on your thumbnail.[8]

How does one deal with such levels of information? We could perhaps use the document retrieval system recommended in this abstract of *The Journal of the American Society for Information Science*: "A probabilistic document-retrieval system may be seen as a sequential learning process, in which the system learns the characteristics of relevant documents, or, more formally, it learns the parameters of probability distributions describing the frequencies of feature occurrences in relevant and nonrelevant documents."[9] Excuse me for a minute while I blow my buffer.

Of course, no one *can* keep up, and we all increasingly realize it. But that doesn't stop us from trying—through more and more education. Which leads to yet another problem.

EDUCATION OVERLOAD?

I won't dispute the value of a good education. How could I? Upon graduation from senior high, I tell my two boys, my schooling was only half finished. After all, part of the Great Commandment is to love the Lord *with all your mind.*

But within the overload context, shouldn't the heretical question be asked: How much education is enough? How much education is too much? Every decade the educational level of the general populace rises. This is linked to better economic well-being and thought in general to lead to a better overall life. I don't disagree. But as the costs in dollars and years of life escalate, we should at least examine our premises. Is education the cure-all we have made it out to be? Or is information overload pushing us to the prophetic fulfillment of ever learning but never arriving at a knowledge of the truth?[10]

For many students, adolescence becomes nothing more than a strenuous competition to get into the best colleges. In an insightful *Newsweek* commentary, high school junior Elizabeth Shaw describes the driven tiredness many students experience.

After a short night's sleep, Elizabeth rises at 6:30 A.M. and stumbles to the bathroom, her eyes puffy. If lucky, she grabs a mouthful of breakfast before her forty-five-minute commute. She naps in class, learns mostly to pass tests, involves herself in an exhausting array of extracurricular activities, and arrives home around 8 P.M., where a lonely microwave dinner awaits. Then, she begins four hours of homework—not interested in understanding, just finishing the assignments. Sometime after midnight she crashes into bed for a few hours of sleep. Shaw relates:

> This cycle continues week after week, broken only by
> weekends full of homework and chores. . . . Why do we do
> this to ourselves? . . . Nearly every high-school student who
> works into the early morning hours is after one thing:
> acceptance to a "good" college. . . . School administrators,
> guidance counselors and parents make it seem as if my life
> will be over unless I get into a good college.

But recently, in talking to other adults, she discovered that most aren't working in their field of study anyway. Furthermore, many had regrets for not enjoying their high school days and their adolescent years when they had the chance. No wonder she asks, "Is This What Life's About?" in the title of her piece.[11]

Is there a difference between getting into a good university and being prepared to live a good life? I think so. Recently, a seventeen-year-old Californian achieved a perfect score on both sections of the SAT. When asked by a reporter, "What is the meaning of life?" she replied, "I have no idea. I would like to know myself."

THE ANTIDOTE FOR DATACIDE

If our brain cells are protesting and our desks are piled high, what can we do about it? Use the following suggestions as a surge protector against information overload and data distress.

Rx 1 *Increase Your Information Selectivity*
Obviously, we cannot read and process all the information we encounter—so how does one decide? Well-thought-out criteria are needed for sorting information into two great piles: that which interests us (or we know should interest us) and everything else. Sort these piles ruthlessly. The bigger the information overload, the more ruthless we need to become.

A high degree of selectivity works best for information services director Mike Rusk, who was receiving twenty technology publications per week. "It was causing me to be frantic. I saw technology moving so fast, at least on paper, and I couldn't keep up with it," he said. For sanity's sake, he decided to cancel all but two of the subscriptions. "I wanted everything to stop so I had time to digest it and see how it fit into our organization."[12]

Don't just wade indiscriminately through huge volumes of material. Be selective. "It is just as absurd for the user to tap the total collection of new material for his data as it would be for the jeweler to order six tons of gold-bearing ore when he wants to make a cufflink," advises Lewis Branscomb.[13]

Rx 2 *Use Interest as an Avenue for Learning*

When we study things we have no affinity for, learning is unavailable. But when we study things we most enjoy, learning is unavoidable.

"Learning can be seen as the acquisition of information, but before it can take place, there must be interest," explains information expert Richard Saul Wurman. "You can't get lost on the road to interest."[14]

The context of learning is all important. "Remembering does not happen as a matter of course whenever a person is exposed to information," states educational theorist Jeremy Campbell. "It does not even happen automatically if the person wants and intends to commit the information to memory. . . . Questions such as how much effort was spent in trying to store it in memory are of surprisingly little importance." Campbell summarizes by stating, "Clearly, meaning is an important ingredient in remembering."[15]

Rx 3 *It Is Okay Not to Know*

Give your brain a break—it is okay to be finite. It is okay not to know everything. For fifteen years my daily job was tutoring young doctors. When asked a question whose answer I did not know, it was always best to admit ignorance. Even when patients asked such questions, my standard answer was, "I'm not sure. Let me ask someone who is smarter than I am." Patients learned to trust me more, not less.

"By giving yourself permission not to know, you can overcome the fear that your ignorance will be discovered," observes Wurman. "When you can admit to ignorance, you will realize that if ignorance isn't exactly bliss, it is an ideal state from which to learn."[16]

Rx 4 *Pitch the Pile*

In nearly every home or office there is a stack of unread journals and magazines. Cancel publications you don't have time to read. Quit stockpiling journals, magazines, newspapers. If you don't have time to read them today, it is purely illusory that you will somehow have time next month.

"It is impossible, unproductive, and unhealthy to try to read everything," observes Marc Ringel, M.D. "In fact, one of the healthiest things you can do, when faced by an enormous, guilt-provoking pile of journals, is to throw them all out and start keeping up again from scratch. The consequences on your career of missing several months of journal articles will be unmeasurable, while the positive effects on your mental health may be considerable. Anything important that was reported in the pile of journals you tossed will reappear in the next pile."[17]

Swenson's suggestion: If the stack is more than six inches high, save the top inch and throw the rest away. If the stack is more than two feet high, throw the whole pile.

Rx 5 *Clear Your Desk*

The average desk worker has thirty-six hours of work on his or her desk and spends three hours a week sorting piles trying to find the project to work on next. Every year the amount of paper metastasizes without pity. We shuffle it around on our desks, stack it next to our easy chair, and pile it high on our shelves. If at all possible OHIO— Only Handle It Once.

A sure sign that you are too busy, according to Scott Buschschacher, is that you clear off your desk by putting everything in a box to look through it later—and you never see the box again. I have a few such boxes. Somewhere. I think.

Rx 6 *Use the Test of Time*

Publishers sometimes contend that the jar of mayonnaise in the refrigerator has a longer half-life than most books. Information pollution has a way of dying a fairly quick natural death. Understanding this, devote time to the works that have stood the "test of time." Read the Bible, the saints, the classics, the best of literature.

Step up a level or two—from data to information to knowledge to wisdom. There is a difference. The further up the line we ascend, the greater the possibility it will stand the test of time.

Rx 7 *Keep an Open Mind*

Some people are regrettably unwilling to deliberate beyond their decision-point. They regard thinking only as a short step on the way to forming an opinion, and sometimes they bypass it altogether. As Matz's Maxim states, a conclusion is the place where you get tired of thinking.

Consider the following two thought lines:

Input ' interpretation ' thinking ' opinion ' end

Often this is the termination of thinking.

Input ' interpretation ' thinking ' opinion ' continued rethinking

This is the ideal case of an open mind.

It is right for us to form opinions and make decisions, but that should not be the end of thinking. We should continue to receive input and be willing to rethink the decision if that is indicated. "A closed mind is a sign of hidden doubt," contends theologian Harold DeWolf.[18]

Rx 8 *Stay Teachable*
As an educator it is possible to assess the teachability quotient of each student. As a pastor or psychologist you can assess the teachability quotient of the person seeking counsel. As a matter of fact, the entire world can probably be divided into two great camps: the teachable and the unteachable. The teachable hold such a massive advantage that I find it hard to measure both camps on the same scale. The unteachable will not grow or develop. The teachable, however, no matter where they began, will have a steady upward course—all the way to God.

Rx 9 *Don't Expect Truth from Information*
In our wired age, information and knowledge bring power and wealth. You can build a career and a fortune on them. But they are inadequate to build a life on.

Don't expect truth from information—they are not the same. Information can only take us so far. For example, when asked about faith, Bill Gates replied, "I don't have enough data on that."

Truth comes not from information, but from revelation. "Sanctify them by the truth," Jesus prayed. "Your word is truth."[19]

Rx 10 *Remain Humble*

Elitism, for me, is one of the most disappointing and discouraging of human sins. And I find it more associated with education than with wealth or politics. Once when I was working short-term in a developing country, another doctor (not American) revealed his disdain for the people we were serving. "Ignorance is the one thing I can't stand," he said. *Arrogance*, I thought, *is the one thing I can't stand.*

As the world increasingly divides into the haves and the have-nots, it will be important to hold the intellectual advantage with humility. Having access to education does not give us any extra credit with God—only increased responsibility.

Rx 11 *Study God's Opinion*

Some people are so overloaded processing information that they have no time left for the Scriptures. My advice is this: Absorb data and study facts, but never neglect God's opinion of the matter. And the journey down the road of God's opinion might lead to a humbling backfire of the intellect. "Do not deceive yourselves," the apostle Paul says. "If any one of you thinks he is wise by the standards of this age, he should become a 'fool' so that he may become wise. For the wisdom of this world is foolishness in God's sight."[20]

In our rush for an education, we all wish to appear learned in the eyes of our peers. But as British author G. K. Chesterton reminds us, "A man who has faith must be prepared not only to be a martyr, but to be a fool."

Rx 12 *Don't Neglect Education of the Heart*

How sad to see people who know the uttermost details of science or the liberal arts but who ignore the matters of the heart. IQ will seldom lead to happiness. Einstein, in fact, once commented, "Those who know the most are the gloomiest."

The Tin Man in *The Wizard of Oz* expressed it well: "Once I had a brain and a heart also. Having tried them both, I should much rather have a heart."

CHAPTER 11

■ ■ ■ ■ ■ ■ ■ ■

Media Overload

■ Right now television has the culture by its throat.
—NEIL POSTMAN

■ In the years ahead, we will live increasingly in fictions: We will turn on our virtual-reality systems and lie back, experiencing heavenly pleasures of sight and sound in a snug electronic nest. The real world will almost be totally blotted out from our experience.—WORLD FUTURE SOCIETY

■ At MTV, we don't shoot for the 14-year-olds, we own them.—BOB PITTMAN, FORMER MTV CHAIRMAN

■ There are no gatekeepers left at the networks.
—BOB GARFIELD, COLUMNIST AT *ADVERTISING AGE*

By now, media in its various forms have penetrated all aspects of contemporary life. It is hard to imagine a life—or even a *single day*—that is not saturated start-to-finish with media. Much of this is acceptable, perhaps even laudable. Movies and television can inform, stimulate, and entertain. Newspapers and magazines keep us up-to-date. Music can lift our spirits, massage our souls, and stimulate our senses. The Internet can, at least potentially, do all of the above.

But everything in a fallen world has a downside. And, in that regard, media is as bad as it gets.

TELEVISION

Anchoring the top spot in the media winner's circle is, of course, the omnipresent television. It has reshaped every aspect of our society, from entertainment to news to political life to religion. It writes its own rules, only partially influenced by viewers.

145

In the average home, the television is turned on seven hours a day. The average viewer watches between twenty and thirty-six hours per week, depending on age and gender. It is hard to over-emphasize the impact of something so temporally dominating.

Some predictions estimate that early into the new millennium, satellite dish technology will be able to deliver five thousand chan-nels. With such cable and satellite access, television's reach into our psyches has not yet peaked. And when you take into account the powerful attractiveness of new technologies such as big screen TVs with HDTV resolution and surround sound, our love affair is not about to end.

MOVIES

The younger the adult age, the more likely we are to be frequent movie attenders or to rent them in videos.

Who does *not* see a movie in the theater in a given month

18-24	seventeen percent
24-34	forty-seven percent
35-44	fifty-seven percent
45-54	sixty-three percent
55-64	seventy-three percent
65 and up	eighty percent[1]

According to media expert Dr. Ted Baehr, teenagers watch fifty movies a year in the theater and view another fifty a year on video. Eighty percent of these movies are PG-13 or R-rated.[2] Research has demonstrated that we store three trillion "videotape" images in our brain by the time we are thirty years old. But, worrisomely, we have no volitional control over selective forgetting. Once the images are there, we must then live with the consequences of that visual imprint. Realizing that the graphic content of R-rated movies is now irrevocably loaded into the memory banks of our youth gives us legitimate cause for alarm.

The easy accessibility of videos has both reshaped and inflated our movie viewing habits. A film is distributed through a sequence of exclusive windows—first in theaters, then in video, pay-per-view, pay TV (such as HBO), basic cable, and finally network television. Movie studios derive more than half of their revenues from video. Even though the video market is facing increasing competition from satellite TV, we rent 3.5 to 4 billion videos a year.[3]

Movies continue their slide in the direction of violence, nudity, and objectionable language. Many blockbuster movies now have elements of all three. The tendency in this direction has been mainstreamed and seems to hardly elicit a yawn.

Children at younger and younger ages are drawn into the movie/video habit, especially with the common use of videos for baby-sitting. As parents become more overloaded, it is simply too tempting to put in a video and place the children before the set. They are well behaved and even entranced. And for busy, stressed-out, exhausted parents, there is nothing so attractive as quiet children.

Toys are now commonly linked to movies that are R-rated. For example, the sci-fi movie *Starship Troopers* has graphic violence, nudity, and objectionable language. Alien bugs impale and behead humans, even sucking out their brains. (This from the same director whose last film was the pornographic NC-17 rated *Showgirls*.) Uninformed parents who see these alien bugs on toy shelves—labeled for kids four and up—are likely to think the movie is acceptable viewing. They would be mistaken.

RADIO, MUSIC, AND CDS

Radio can be a wonderful companion on the road, in the lonely hours of the night, or—for that matter—at *any* hour. Music, the mainstay of radio programming, is a special gift from the creative genius of God. Unfortunately, it has been counterclaimed by the Evil One, and the battle rages furiously for the heart and soul of a nation—especially our youth.

Records ruled the music world until 1982, when sales were eclipsed for the first time by audiocassettes. In 1992, CDs passed cassettes. The unique captivating power of music somehow results in discordant, strident melodies with shocking lyrics selling millions overnight, including such themes as sexual obsession, incest, rape, dehumanized sex, mutilation, cop-killing, torture, dismemberment, suicide, self-loathing, and nihilism.[4] (Specific examples are included in the Notes for those interested—and able to tolerate it.) How did we arrive at such a place? This much we know: Time Warner granted generous assistance along the way.

To assume that the average American teenager has not heard these songs is to be culturally naive. As Gerald Early has pointed out, "There is no innocence in childhood, only less mature depravities."[5] The average parent, however, remains blissfully unaware. "Teenagers receive at least two dozen forms of entertainment," explains media expert Bob DeMoss, "and most of it flies under the radar screen of adults."[6]

INTERNET AND COMPUTERS

Is the Internet (called *anarchy that works*) rightly considered a medium? Increasingly, the answer must be yes. It informs, entertains, advertises. And it is explosive. No one can completely predict how dominant it will become, just as no one really predicted its advent or its rapid ascension. Analysts expect forty-three percent of U.S. households to have some Internet capability by the year 2000.[7]

"Computer cost effectiveness has risen 100 millionfold since the late 1950s—a 100 thousandfold rise in power times a thousandfold drop in cost," explains technology expert George Gilder. "Three years ago, all the phone networks in the world combined carried an average of a terabit a second. Today, [individual] companies are sending three terabits per second down a single fiber thread the width of a human hair."[8] When you combine this stunning development with the anticipated growth in satellite technology—both geostationary (GEOs) and low-earth-orbiting (LEOs) satellites—estimates of Internet users vary from 300 million to 1 billion at the turn of the millennium.[9]

Kids can often navigate the Internet better than their parents, who never quite know what their children are into. Additionally, this trend can be socially isolating. In one survey, forty-six percent of respondents said their children prefer computers to their peers.[10]

Pornography over the Internet is, in my opinion, the greatest moral threat ever encountered in the pornography arena. It is more private than ever before and will prove to be far more devastating than most people can imagine. Speaking of the Internet, Bill Maher of television's *Politically Incorrect* explains, "Anything you can put sex into will be used for that purpose more than for anything else."[11] One adult entertainment website, ClubLove, reported an estimated 1.4 *billion* hits in 1997.

Computers once made great claims for the potential of CD-ROMs. But they are experiencing a type of overloading trouble all their own. With about ten thousand titles available, people simply do not have the time nor money to shop through these offerings. And even if they did, they do not have the time to use such a vast array of capacity. The essence of CD-ROM still shows great promise. But here, just as in any other area, too much is too much. Ultimately, overload brings us all to our knees.

EFFECTS OF MEDIA OVERLOAD

Media has reordered social thought and behavior in unprecedented ways. The widespread effects of this media profusion are broadly integrative, thus rendering the following discussion only partial.

Resets the Moral Acceptability Threshold

"Do the things that once offended you now entertain you?" asks media critic Al Menconi. "Are you able to enjoy the company of television programs, videos, and movies that have values diametrically opposed to yours? . . . Do you remember the first time you heard someone use profanity in a motion picture? I do. It was less than twenty years ago, in the movie "All the President's Men." I was shocked that they could use that word. Now we hear worse on television every night."[12]

This moral drift is important to understand, for it continues unabated. Extrapolate ten or twenty years into the future and it is frightening to imagine what media content awaits us.

Resets the Shock Threshold

In the past, if we saw blood, killing, or tragedies on the evening news, it would disturb us for weeks. Today, however, the rule of the newsroom is, "If it bleeds, it leads."

Movies are worse. Beginning about thirty years ago, succeeding waves of movies relied on more and more violence to attract crowds. Audiences became numbed to the repulsiveness of each level of violence, so directors had to enhance the horror to maintain interest. Such common fare no longer elicits anguish. To be sure, there is a temporary adrenaline kick — the kind that causes you to eat your popcorn faster. But no anguish.

Resets the Boredom Threshold

After one eight-year-old boy had been watching television all Saturday afternoon, his father politely asked him to turn off the set. When five minutes of silence had elapsed, the boy moaned, "But Dad, it's so lonely."

Results in Addictive Behavior

As a generalization, when media is available, people use it as a first option — the younger the age, the truer this principle holds. And once fully indoctrinated into this world of media, it is hard to break away. Media increasingly defines our world, and taking the media away is like taking our world away. When media is gone, there is seemingly nothing left — no inner reality, no relationships, no comfort, laughter, music, or security.

Gives a More Negative View of the World

The world is already in enough trouble and we don't need to make it appear any worse than it is. But in the world of media, bad news sells. According to media critic Ben Wattenberg, bad news is big news. Additionally, good news is no news. So if you want to get on the air, the formula is the simple: Say something terrible.[13]

Fictional programming isn't any better than the newscasts. The average prime-time TV schedule presents the viewer with 350 characters each night, seven of whom will be murdered on screen. "If this rate applied in reality, then in just 50 days, everyone in the United States would be killed," explains media critic Michael Medved.[14]

Increases Exposure to Sexual Material

The pervasiveness of media leads to an almost unavoidable exposure to sexually explicit material at ever-younger ages. Observes adolescent medicine specialist Victor Strasburger, M.D.:

> Teenagers watch an average of three hours of TV per day, listen to the radio for an additional one to two hours, and often have access to R-rated movies and even pornography long before they are adults. According to the best study from the late 1980s, the average American teenager views almost 15,000 sexual jokes, innuendoes and other references on TV each year. Fewer than 170 of these deal with what any sane adult would define as responsible sexual behavior. . . . Add to that the 20,000 commercials per year each teenager in America sees—with implicit messages that sex is fun, sex is sexy and everyone out there is having sex but you—and you have at least the possibility of a fairly important influence.[15]

WHAT IS AHEAD?

In the future, people will increasingly live in their home media centers where their alternative reality will be irresistibly more enjoyable than the stressful realities of work and relationships. They will have a seven-foot high, two-inch thick high-resolution screen hanging on the wall connected to their television/computer/Internet/phone/cable/satellite complex. With easy and secure credit card payment mechanisms, they will be able to browse hundreds (or thousands) of television channels, call in any movie they wish when they wish it, surf the Internet, or shop to their heart's content.

Additionally, many will choose a virtual-reality sex life on demand. Health authorities and social welfare advocates might even propose cybersex as a cost-effective solution for the costly epidemics of unwanted pregnancies, abortion, sexually-transmitted diseases and AIDS.[16] If this scenario bothers you as much as it does me, begin preparing answers now. It will be here sooner than you think.

PRESCRIPTIONS FOR MODERATING MEDIA SATURATION

A passive approach to media consumption is not only unwise but increasingly irresponsible. The following are suggestions and guidelines that will help steer a healthy course through a risky minefield.

Rx 1 *Guard Against Media Constituting Your Only Barrier to Loneliness*

It is easy to lapse into a *media-saturated* existence, which eventually leads to a *media-dependent* existence. When lonely, bored, or stressed, the first thing we often do is activate our media surroundings—which usually means turning on the television. In a previous era, we would instead have perhaps visited a friend.

If you are lonely, get in the car and visit someone who would welcome the contact. Or get on the phone and call a friend. Write a letter of encouragement. Invite someone over. Make a coffee date.

This is not to say that all such media usage for loneliness is inappropriate. But if overused, it will result in more isolation, not less.

Rx 2 *Allow Boredom to Nourish the Imagination*

Don't fear boredom—it can be useful. People can't stand it for long. Boredom is a seed bed of imagination. To short-circuit boredom is to short-circuit creativity.

The temptation is to solve boredom with media. If the children are bored, don't always turn to TV, videos, or computer games. Let the boredom build. If boredom increases with no possibility of electronics, imagination will begin to surface. This is called "play." Play is the business of childhood. Let kids get bored and have to play their way out of it.

"What could have been long periods of super stagnation (stranded in a hayfield in the heat of August and cow-sitting!) forced us to hatch up our own amusements," explains Edna Hong, in describing her growing up years. "What we hatched proves among other things the creative power inherent in boredom, of being placed in a situation so boring that the most fallow imagination begins to improve."[17]

Rx 3 *Create Rather than Consume*
Life is meant to be participatory and relational. As James Coleman explained, "Life in general used to be experience-rich and stimulus-poor; now it has become nearer the reverse."[18]

Create entertainment, don't just consume it. Prefer active over passive. Play the football game yourself. Make your own music. Visit, bake, sew together. Travel. Don't live a vicarious virtual-reality existence. Instead, create a personal-experience reality.

Rx 4 *Establish Media Limits*
If media in all its forms continues to escalate in visibility and dominance, there obviously comes a point when we have to impose limits. Decide such limits as an act of intention rather than randomness.

For example, consider putting some limits on television. It is acceptable for TV to be an interlude, but it should not become a way of life. Have standard rules that make sense. Don't force yourselves into re-deciding every week. *Possible* suggestions (not laws!) might include:

- ■ Allow up to seven hours of TV (including videos) each week.
- ■ Require all viewing to be preplanned or intentional.
- ■ No TV is allowed until homework or chores are done.
- ■ One hour per day can be viewed only for approved shows.

Also limit the number of channels—be leery about expanding. More is not necessarily *better.* Limit the number of TVs as well. Although the majority of children today have a television in their own room (fifty-eight percent), mostly it is not a good idea. For one reason, we want to live as a family—otherwise "home is where we live alone together." For another reason, it is essential that parents keep an eye on what their children watch.

Beyond television, consider also establishing limits on Nintendo, Sega, Walkman, and Internet use.

Rx 5 *Have Non-electronic Children's Parties*
Consider not renting or viewing any electronics for birthdays or slumber parties. Cultivate other activities instead. For our boys'

birthdays, we would always have two special events: marshmallow fights (they are safe and don't hurt) and darts thrown at balloons. Each balloon contained a small note with promises of a treat. The participant would pick up the note and immediately collect the treat. Later, we used an Ecuadorian blowgun instead of darts.

The point is, it is possible to have fun without the media dominating the scene. But once media is introduced, forget it. Nothing else can compete.

Rx 6 *Resist Advertisements*

Ads are omnipresent in our "engineered-message" lives. If we try to completely avoid them, we will not succeed. The next best thing is to discipline ourselves and train our children to be wary. Point out the falsehood and manipulation in each ad. Teach discernment. Distinguish between advertising "information" and "propaganda." Talk about the enormous cost of ads, thus their power. If ads don't influence, why are companies willing to pay millions of dollars for a few seconds of exposure? Discuss contentment versus discontentment. Talk about "need-creation." Ask yourself and the family, "If God were sitting on the couch with us, what would He think of this ad?"

My habit is either to turn the channel during ads, or mute it and get something else accomplished.

Rx 7 *Zap the Set*

Consider always having the remote nearby when watching television. Use it freely. Also use it as a threat and a teaching tool. If something objectionable comes on, hit the mute button, switch the channel, or turn off the set.

As violence screening chips (V-chips) were first being discussed, one man told me he had his own V-chip. He would sit on the couch with an open scissors, through which coursed an extension cord to the television. His children would stare at him with wide-eyed wonder, fearful that he might actually cut the power when inappropriate material came on the screen. I hope he does. Often. It would be a visible lesson the children would not soon forget.

Rx 8 *Disconnect Cable Selectively*
If you have cable—and most people do—there are some things best to avoid. Most cable operators will allow selective disconnection from those elements that you find objectionable. When I asked media expert Bob DeMoss if there was any reason people should have HBO and MTV in their homes, his answer was immediate: "None."

Popular movie critic Michael Medved agrees: "There is absolutely no excuse for MTV to be present in the home," he maintains. "It is one hundred percent negative."[19]

Call your carrier and request they selectively discontinue such channels from your cable package.

Rx 9 *Fast from the Media*
Throughout this book, the notion of modern *fasting* occurs often. Media is perhaps one of the most important kinds of fasts. Have a *no-television* week or month. Don't listen to the news perhaps for a week. Pray in the car instead of listening to the radio. Or simply enjoy the silence for a change. Cancel the newspaper or magazine. Create an intentional solitude.

Rx 10 *Regain Control of the Value System*
"Parents can no longer control the atmosphere of the home and have even lost the will to do so," asserted Professor of Social Thought Allan Bloom in *The Closing of the American Mind*.[20] Sadly, many of us have essentially and tragically lost control of the value system of our children—often compliments of the media. If we still hope to influence them in the direction of virtue, it is important to make our move early.

Spend time watching television and movies with your children. Be aware of what movies they are watching, what music they are listening to, what television programs are their favorites. Make an effort to understand their views and values. Discern their evolving worldview. (It *is* evolving—it's just that they don't always discuss it with their parents). Take pains to influence (without being overly paternalistic or preachy) while you still have the opportunity—you will lose control soon enough.

When your kids are young, have their friends play at your house so you can know what they are watching. Also let them know it is okay to call you to pick them up at any hour if they are at a friend's house and feel uncomfortable about the television or video selection.

Rx 11 *Be Aware*

We cannot effectively confront a problem in our society until we understand it. Yet to understand contemporary media requires that we watch and listen to very disturbing television, movie, and musical material. What to do? It presents a difficult dilemma plaguing many: either ignore the existence of such disturbing content, thus rendering ourselves ill-equipped to understand the needs of our children and neighbors; or expose ourselves to such content and thus subject ourselves to contamination. It is like asking: Should we eat garbage or go hungry?

Personally I have chosen to peruse some of what is out there, partly because of my work as a cultural analyst and futurist. For the general populace, however, I do not have an easy answer. Yet *somehow* we need to be more aware if we wish to understand and influence those around us.

Rx 12 *Hate Evil*

Evil, for reasons not completely clear to me, is always more interesting. This obviously is not a statement about the way things should be, but simply a statement of the way things are. Once we understand this, much that is mysteriously wrong in life becomes clearer. For example, if we had forty-nine stations broadcasting healthy, virtuous programming, and only one station broadcasting violent or sexual programming, most of America would be tuned into the one channel. Even church people. Evil is always more interesting.

Understanding the allure of evil explains why we watch so much of it, even when it is so clearly destructive. The sheer volume of evil our nation is exposed to on a daily basis is one of the most disturbing effects of the proliferation of media. The only remedy I know is two thousand years old: "Hate what is evil; cling to what is good."[21]

Rx 13 *Take the Internet Plunge*
It might surprise some to hear me suggest getting on-line. Internet access is virtually inevitable for all homes — just as were the telephone, television, and microwave. A balanced understanding of the age in which we live includes thinking through such new technologies rather than rejecting them out of hand.

The Internet will solve some problems and will exacerbate others. But there is no stopping it. We should not boycott it because of its downside but rather use it with care and discretion.

So sign on, but be careful. I have three main concerns:

■ It can be a waste of time — set up guidelines.
■ It can lead to addictive behavior — guard against it.
■ It can give almost unlimited access to pornography in a much more dangerous way than ever before — install screening devices against inappropriate sites.

Rx 14 *Substitute Soothing Music*
Music fills the air and the ears of America, especially our youth. For many youth (perhaps most), music heroes have even greater stature than movie or sports stars. To simply tell these kids to stop listening is not realistic — they won't. But if we can give them an alternative, perhaps. . . . At least we can try. And hope. And pray.

Looking beyond the interests of our children to our preferences, there is a wide choice of what we might listen to. My advice: Listen to that which calms the spirit.

Rx 15 *Use a Movie Viewer Guide*
Many movies today are unfit for viewing — but which ones? To help discern, our family subscribes to a movie preview guide to make sure the movie meets our personal standards for acceptability. The guide lists acceptability ratings from -4 to +4, and entertainment ratings from 0 to 4. Their report also lists objectionable elements in each movie, so there are few surprises in the middle of the movie. We have established certain minimum acceptability guides. This way the boys' displeasure at our restriction is displaced onto the guide rather than on us. Having a concrete guide

prevents a power struggle with each movie. It might seem a bit expensive, but we have found it invaluable.

Here are two possible guides to choose from:

■ *Preview* comes out twice a month, and costs $33/year. 1309 Seminole Drive, Richardson, TX 75080 (Phone: 972-231-9910)
■ *MovieGuide* comes out twice a month, and new subscriptions cost $15.95 for 6 months or $28.88 for one year. Address: Good News Communications, P.O. Box 190010, Atlanta, GA 31119 (Phone: 800-899-6684)

Rx 16 *Rent Videos*

Watching a movie together can be a valuable bonding experience. But at today's prices it costs $25 to $30 to take a family of four to the theater. Renting a video instead (or checking it out at the library for free or a minimal charge) has many advantages: it is less expensive; you can discuss the movie as it progresses; you can turn it off if it becomes objectionable; you can pause to get a snack or use the bathroom; and the popcorn doesn't cost $3.

Establishing a warm atmosphere in the home for such an event is a treat the children will long remember. In our family, we often will turn off the telephones, light candles, have a fire in the fireplace, enjoy special snacks, and push the sofas together.

Preview publishes an updated Family Video Guide of one thousand recommended videos. It provides a synopsis of the plot, suggested age for viewing, and entertainment rating.

Rx 17 *Encourage Reading*

Someone once said, "Having your book made into a movie is like having your oxen made into bouillon cubes." A good book well written is almost always superior to the corresponding movie. The book's language is more creative than the movie script, and the mind's imagination is usually more interesting than the movie set.

Consider reading the book together instead of seeing the movie. Or perhaps do both. The goal is not only to entertain, but to teach children a love for the written word. To accomplish such a lofty purpose in the face of overwhelming competition from movies and television requires more than coercion. It should be warmly relational as well. "It's the quality of interaction between the parent and child, or teacher and child, that motivates the kids in reading," explains psychologist Carrie Becker.[22]

In our family, the children were "invested" readers—meaning we bribed them. Not paying an allowance, we instead offered to pay a penny a page for reading books. After the title, author, and number of pages were recorded they were paid. When they wanted to make a special purchase, such as a bicycle or outdoor equipment, they would "read" for it. As a side benefit, avid readers usually limit their electronic media time.

Rx 18 *Create a Reading Evening*
Consider having a regular or episodic family reading evening. Go through a book or series together, such as C. S. Lewis's *Chronicles of Narnia* or J. R. R. Tolkien's *Lord of the Rings* trilogy. Or have each person reading his or her own book, but be together while doing it. Make it a special evening, with favorite food, snacks, soda, or juice. Create a warm, quiet, uninterrupted atmosphere. Announce it days in advance—don't spring it on the kids last-minute.

Rx 19 *Visit Used Bookstores*
More than two billion new books are purchased each year in the U.S., among them the 58,000 new titles that appear annually. But it can also be great fun to visit used bookstores. What a thrill to find an out-of-print classic for $1.50, or a recent twenty dollar hardbound best seller for three dollars. Linda has enjoyed searching for books by the British author Elizabeth Goudge, and we now are working toward completing our collection of her wonderful, otherwise unavailable works. Many libraries sponsor quarterly used book sales. One suggestion is to inquire about the sale dates and pencil them in on the calendar as a scheduled event.

Rx 20 *Have a Family Outing*
The library is as enjoyable a place to visit as the movies—but only if you start young enough. Our library is nestled on the shores of a

beautiful lake, with window seats next to the water. It is hard to imagine a better setting to come for a quiet family outing. When the kids were younger, we also would go to used bookstores for family activities. They had no trouble entertaining themselves looking among the shelves that contained material of interest to them. Walks, hikes, fishing, museums, zoos, car rides into the country—all are satisfying alternatives for a life of media overload. Once the children are older, they will resist. That's okay, they will still have memories—an important legacy that will later serve them well.

Rx 21 *Include Only the Best*

Be selective about what media you allow in your home or into your life. There is so much to choose from and so much that is harmful, it seems unnecessary to even discuss the notion of choosing only what is best. But busyness and overload often overwhelm common sense, let alone discernment.

For television, choose only the best. For example, how can anyone go wrong with "Anne of Green Gables"? When our children were younger, we would watch *Little House on the Prairie* together. Even today these evenings remain as some of our fondest memories. Watch programming that models relational reconciliation and godly problem-solving. There is no controversy involved in watching the things that are noble and relationally powerful.

CHAPTER 12

■ ■ ■ ■ ■ ■ ■

Possession

■ In the next twenty-five years, the world's system will pro-
duce more goods than all of previous history of the world
combined.—BARRY ASMUS, ECONOMIST

■ Be content with what you've got; and be sure you've got
plenty.—HAGAR'S TWO RULES FOR HAPPINESS

■ He who buys what he doesn't need steals from himself.
—SWEDISH PROVERB

■ A man's life does not consist in the abundance of his possessions.—JESUS, LUKE 12:15

Years ago in Siam, if the king had an enemy he wanted to torment,
it was easy: Give him a white elephant. The receiver of this gift
was now obligated into oblivion. Any gift from the king obviously had to be cared for—it could not be given away without
causing offense. Additionally, a white elephant was considered
sacred and thus required the best nourishment and protection.
Soon the extreme costs of caring for the gift drove the king's enemy
to destitution.

Today it seems everyone in America is on the king's hit list. We
are increasingly buried under mountains of possessions. Closets
are full, attics are groaning, garages are bulging, storage space is saturated. Swollen houses lead to the three-car-garage syndrome: huge
homes with spacious garages, yet all the cars parked in the driveway because the garages are already full.

If that little space left in your house is creating an annoying sucking sound, there is no shortage of consumer clutter waiting to occupy
the temporary vacuum. For example, if you have $1.2 million to $75

161

million, you could buy a personal submarine over the Internet from the U.S. government (www.ussubs.com). Or you could buy a lighted Christmas wreath for the front grill of your car. If you want to light up the life of someone special, you can spend $400,000 for the Heartthrob Brooch. It has six rubies, seventy-eight diamonds, and chip-controlled, light-emitting diodes which flash with each beat of the wearer's heart. Or you could purchase the world's smallest working model railroad with a nineteen-inch attaché case for only $1,295 (battery included). If you buy sterling silver thermometer cufflinks for $98, you can take the temperature of your wrists.

If you can't find it at the mall, try mail order. *The Catalog of Catalogs* lists more than twelve thousand catalogs from which to order. "I hope you will not only find what you are looking for, but also hundreds of other teasers you'll want to send away for," writes the editor. "Don't resist the urge!" One of their best selling catalogs is "Things You Never Knew Existed" — *Items you can't possibly live without!*

CONSUMER ORGY

"Affluenza," states the PBS television special, "is an unhappy condition of overload, debt, anxiety, and waste resulting from the dogged pursuit of more." Affluenza turns the *good* life into the *goods* life. We now have more shopping malls than high schools, and in many communities, the mall has become the center of community life. Mall mania leads to recreational shopping, compulsive shopping, and therapeutic shopping. As many as one-third of shoppers express an irresistible compulsion to buy—often in reaction to stress, anxiety, or depression. Forty percent of these compulsive shoppers admit their closets are filled with unopened items. Thomas O'Guinn, professor of advertising, University of Illinois, believes that "consumers are in an endless, hopeless search for happiness through the acquisition of things."[1]

Not only do we want more—we want bigger. Not just quantity, but bulk. Houses are three rooms larger than they were twenty years ago, even though families are smaller. Our cars are bigger, shoes are larger, furniture is overstuffed, tubs are huge, and now they have a mattress one size up from the king. Plates even hold more, McDonald's tells us to *Supersize it!*, and 7-Eleven has a 64 ounce *Double Gulp*. "We're having a harmonic convergence for bigness," observes Jon Berry, editor of *Public Pulse*.

Florida attorney Stacey Giulianti is a case in point. "I've got a 61-inch TV, which, diagonally, is one inch bigger than my own mother," the twenty-nine-year-old lawyer said. "I've got an 11-speaker surround-sound system. I've got oversized plush couches and a monster-size kitchen with a huge bread maker and a commercial-size mixer. And I've got a large master bedroom with a walk-in closet that was the size of my bedroom in my old house." He has a soaking tub, twelve-foot cathedral ceilings and an enormous Infiniti four-by-four truck that they never drive off-road. "Life is messy," he points out, "and it's nice when you're done with your day to be able to come home and soak in the big tub, grill in your big backyard, and watch your 61-inch TV. It allows you to escape the daily stress. You work hard, you want to enjoy your comforts."[2]

Where is one to store this cultural largess? In ever larger houses, of course. Martha Stewart, after all, has to put her sixteen televisions someplace. One Californian mansion we saw from a distance has twenty bedrooms, twenty-five bathrooms, plus both indoor and outdoor Olympic size pools for a thirty-two-year-old man, his wife, and daughter. Ironically, he made a fortune in the mini-storage business.

Today, many garages are as large as entire houses were in the 1950s. Forget Martha's TVs; Jerry Seinfeld has to put his sixty cars somewhere.

INEXTINGUISHABLE NEEDS

I suppose there was a time, several decades back, when both manufacturers and retailers feared a theoretical saturation point—that threshold where consumers would say *enough* and stop buying. But if they ever feared the existence of such a theoretical point, by now the answer has declared itself: There is no such point of satiety. No matter how much people have, they still want more.

"The urgency of wants does not diminish appreciably as more

of them are satisfied," explained John Kenneth Galbraith in *The Affluent Society.* "When man has satisfied his physical needs, then psychologically grounded desires take over. These can never be satisfied or, in any case, no progress can be proved."[3] Forty years after he wrote those words, his economic theory still holds. "So long as the consumer adds new products—seeks variety rather than quantity—he may accumulate without diminishing the urgency of his wants" Galbraith summarizes.[4]

PRESCRIPTIONS FOR CURBING THE CLUTTER

If you are looking up at your mountain of possessions from a deep hole of debt, rather than rent another storage garage consider the following suggestions.

Rx 1 *See Owning as a Liability Rather than an Asset*
There seems to be a one-to-one relationship between the *possession of things* and *the consumption of time.* Everything we own requires a commitment of our work time to pay for it and our leisure time to use and care for it. Don't buy or keep anything if the time spent on it competes unfavorably with family, service, or God. Remember: Everything we own owns us. We are free in accordance with the number of things we can do without.

At the beginning of every day we are given assignments with eternal significance—to serve and to love. But when God issued these assignments, He wasn't intending that we serve things and love possessions. He was talking about people. The simpler our possessions, the more time for people.

Rx 2 *Unclutter*
Life is busy enough, days are interrupted enough, and space is crowded enough. Whenever we get a chance, it is wise to kick out the clutter.

"Getting rid of it all was a tremendously liberating experience," relates simplicity author Elaine St. James. "Once you begin to experience the exhilaration and the sense of freedom such an exercise generates, uncluttering will become easier and easier."[5] Until you come into that sense of exhilaration you may need a "clutter buddy," defined as "one who supports another person in sorting and discarding accumulated personal possessions."[6]

Rx 3 *Have a Birthday Party*

"I've proven that I can make what I need to make, buy what I need to buy," said New York writer Liz Perle McKenna. "What I own doesn't say who I am anymore." So for her fortieth birthday party, she asked her guests to come to her home and take something away.[7]

Rx 4 *Look Down the Ladder*

Instead of looking *up the ladder* at people who have possessions we lack, Joni Eareckson Tada teaches us to change the direction of our gaze — look *down the ladder* at the poor, the ill, the destitute. Imagine ourselves in their shoes. When, through compassion, we internalize their hardship, it will deliver us from our current bondage to envy. The *desire for more* is replaced by the *gratitude for enough*.

Rx 5 *Resist the Consumptive Lifestyle*

In modern America, living a consumptive lifestyle is as natural as breathing. To *shop till you drop* is thoroughly and thoughtlessly mainstream. People are temporarily pleased with their external purchases but chronically unhappy with their internal emptiness. To step off the treadmill requires a level of understanding, of intention, of resistance that is hard to come by. No one models it for us, and we don't have the time or energy to think through the implications and consequences on our own.

All that is rapidly changing. At an unprecedented pace, voluntary simplicity is gaining enthusiastic adherents. Is it possible that the most important answers for our most important problems are not consumption-based answers? Christ's chosen lifestyle two millennia ago gave a prominent hint as to God's opinion on this issue.

Rx 6 *Make a List*

A large percentage of purchases are bought on impulse. Fifty percent of hardware purchases, for example, are impulse decisions — as are fifty percent of grocery purchases. Impulse purchases are those things we didn't go to the store to buy—but we bought anyway.

Make a list of needed items *before* going to the store. Don't leave home without it and don't deviate from it.

Rx 7 *Be Creative*

One of the difficulties with our hyperliving, exhausted, chronically-behind lifestyle is that often we must buy our way out of hurriedness: quickly pick up that present at full price and pay to have it gift-wrapped; stop for fast food once again tonight; place a call to hire someone to pull off the birthday party.

A simpler, slower pace to life pays many dividends, not the least of which is a newfound ability to use creativity to solve our problems instead of money. "We try to come up with a creative solution," explains Elaine St. James, "rather than a buying solution."[8]

Rx 8 *Stay Off the Treadmill*

Harvard economist Juliet Schor explains how, instead of an earn-and-save cycle, most Americans have adopted a work-and-spend cycle. This involves a nonstop and accelerating treadmill of working more, wanting more, buying more, owing more, and then working more again.

If we buy expensive houses and automobiles, obviously these purchases need to be paid for. Things are paid for in dollars; dollars are earned by working; working consumes time; and time is what we are trying to gain. Therefore, *fewer things = less work = more time.*

Rx 9 *Counter the Culture with Like-minded Friends*

Culture is not a passive agent in our possession problem but instead a powerful force that demands we buy its wares and live by its rules. Acquiescing to such demands inevitably leads to overload and margin erosion. Many of these cultural expectations wither under the scrutiny of Scripture, yet we willingly subject ourselves to their control.

When Linda and I made our dramatic lifestyle change, we asked God to redesign our lives according to that which was spiritually authentic. Because God's opinion is always the healthy option, our redesigned life indeed turned out to be healthier and more satisfying than the life we were leading under the tutelage of culture.

God tells us we cannot be conformed to the world and be free at the same time. "Do not conform any longer to the pattern of this world," the apostle Paul declares, "but be transformed by the renewing of your mind."[9] In other words, Christians who desire freedom must become a "contrast-society." This does not mean we drop out but simply that we refuse societal servitude.

Willingly and knowingly we wrestle control from culture and set our orientation in the opposite direction. It is wonderful if a community of believers can support one another in making such countercultural decisions. The more different we are from the ambient culture, the more we need to be surrounded by like-minded friends who will support our value structure.

Rx 10 Pass It Around

The idea of owning some things in common is both practical and biblical. Why should each family own its own canoe, Rototiller, chain saw, and food dehydrator? When we share graciously the things God has given us, the blessing flows to others. It helps contain the clutter, ease the debt burden, and build community.

Rx 11 Redefine Happiness

"Grandma, I just found out what happiness is. It's that feeling you have just after you buy something." Vicki Robin, coauthor of *Your Money or Your Life,* relates overhearing this from a four-year-old. And yet how many of our children—at least superficially—believe in the same creed? Indeed, how many of us often share the same feelings?

Happiness comes from being loved and knowing truth. To convince our children of this reality—to say nothing of a watching world—will require more than preaching. It will require a lifestyle consistent with our definition.

Rx 12 Change Your Value System

In the context of possessions, there are three important rules about values. The first is that people are more important than things. The second is that people are more important than things. And the third is that people are more important than things.

In my study is a calligraphy that Linda commissioned, containing a passage from Dickens' *Bleak House*. It is the testimony of an unusually virtuous woman who, in the end, marries the tender-hearted physician. "We are not rich in the bank, but we have always prospered and have quite enough," Esther says contentedly. "I never walk out with my husband, but I hear the people bless him. I never go into a house of any degree, but I hear his praises, or see them in grateful eyes. I never lie down at night, but I know that in the course of the day he has alleviated pain, and soothed some fellow-creature in the time of need. I know that from the beds of those who were past recovery, thanks have often, often gone up, in the last hour, for his patient ministration. Is not this to be rich?"[10]

Simple words from a simple life. But, indeed, who could wish for more? If we but valued what Esther valued, she would lead us away from a life of worry, envy, and clutter into a life of freedom, joy, and service.

Rx 13 *Forget the Joneses*

Life in America has become essentially a comparative experience. We are not content or discontent in accordance with what we have—we are content or discontent in accordance with what our neighbor has. Stop looking at the Joneses—they are partly responsible for getting us into this mess. As an act of intention, let's turn our eyes away from our neighbors. "If you get into the comparison game," warns Tim Kimmel, "the world will *eat your lunch*."

Rx 14 *Change Your Lifestyle*

Some people are so exhausted, stressed, breathless, and indebted that they appropriately decide to work less and slow down. The only problem is—they forget to change their lifestyle.

If we are serious about making changes to address overload, there must be commensurate lifestyle change. Largely, it seems to me, such a lifestyle change will require a change in the way we use and value possessions. Instead of a life defined by the cultivation of things, it will be a life given over to deeper, more transcendent issues of the spirit.

Rx 15 *Decide Your Possession End-Point*

In America, says Russ Crosson, "We tend to measure success with a *thingometer.*" But how many possessions are enough? Seldom do we address this important issue in specific, objectively measurable ways. "The concept of satiation has very little standing in economics," explains John Kenneth Galbraith. "The more wants that are satisfied the more new ones are born."[11] While these statements are clearly true in culture at large, they should never be true in our individual lives, for this is the picture of chronic discontent.

Think specifically about satiety and contentment. How much money do we need to make? Write it down. What kind of car will we be satisfied with? Write it down. How many suits do we need? How much will we spend on shoes? How often do we need expensive cuts of meat? Write it down.

Let's not write down the answers for our neighborhoods. This is a private issue between us and God.

Rx 16 *Make Room*

In Tolstoy's *War And Peace,* Napoleon is marching on Moscow in 1812. Within a few days, the city is doomed to fall, so all the people are busy packing their possessions to evacuate.

One wealthy count has more than thirty carts loaded with furniture and valuables in the courtyard of his mansion. But also in the courtyard and lining the streets of the city are wounded soldiers, waiting inevitable death at the hands of Napoleon's advancing army. Suddenly, the count's daughter sees it: possessions on the carts to be rescued; wounded people on the ground left to die. With tears in her eyes, she runs to her father, pleading to put the wounded on the carts. The count, who has a tender heart as well, sees the shame of it. Weeping, he hugs his daughter: "The eggs are teaching the chickens."

The count quickly tells the servants to take the possessions off and put the wounded on. The servants, who one minute before were doing "the only thing there was to do"—loading the possessions—were now doing the "only thing that could be done"—taking possessions off the carts and putting people on.[12]

What is on our carts? Possessions? Things that consume both our time and money? Things that are temporal, perishable, here today and gone tomorrow? May we have the grace to unclutter our carts to make room for that which matters most.

CHAPTER 13

■ ■ ■ ■ ■ ■ ■ ■

Work

■ Work expands to fill the time available.—PARKINSON'S LAW

■ All junior executives should know that if they work hard ten hours a day, every day, they could be promoted to senior executives so that they can work hard for fourteen hours a day.—JOHN CAPOZZI

■ Leslie works part-time. That way, she has plenty of time left over to be busy.—TIM KIMMEL

■ We are frequently asked if it is possible to "have it all"—a full satisfying personal life and a full and satisfying, hard-working professional one. Our answer is: NO. . . . Excellence is a high cost item.—TOM PETERS

The turn of the millennium is witnessing an unprecedented era of high job creation and low unemployment. Since 1980, even though the U.S. economy has *lost* more than forty million jobs, at least seventy million new jobs have been *created*. Currently, we have a record 122 million jobs in the U.S. The economy's updrafts have created not only new jobs, but also new products, new services, new industries, new global markets, new millionaires, and new stock market records.

Yet, during this same stretch, the economy experienced down drafts as well. For many workers, hours are long, wages are low, benefits are fading, pace is fast, stress is unmanageable, morale is down, and security is threatened. One in six workers admits that he or she thinks about quitting on a weekly basis.[1] At one high-tech company, an executive was given a cynical standing ovation when he announced long-expected layoffs with severance packages. For these frustrated employees, Dilbert was no joke.

Work is obviously God-ordained. A life without meaningful

work is a tragic life. Each person is healthier—as the entire society is healthier—if we have appropriate, fulfilling work that can be done with pride and integrity. "As our ancestors have known," explains British economist E. F. Schumacher, "there can be no joy of life without joy of work."[2] But work overload is a different matter entirely. It is, like all other overloads, destructive.

OVERWORKING

The Japanese have a death-by-overwork syndrome called *karoshi* where otherwise healthy men simply drop dead at their desks. Yet a recent international study reveals that the Japanese do not lead the world in work hours—the U.S. does.

NUMBER OF HOURS WORKED ANNUALLY, 1995[3]

Country	Number of working hours
USA	1,896
Switzerland	1,838
Japan	1,832
Spain	1,772
United Kingdom	1,762
France	1,755
Italy	1,720
Netherlands	1,717
Eastern Germany	1,705
Western Germany	1,602

Harvard economist Juliet Schor, whose book *The Overworked American* sparked a national discussion, explains that in the last twenty years, the average U.S. worker has added the equivalent of one month to the work-year. Berkeley sociologist and work trends author Arlie Hochschild notes that today women are working, on average, 41.7 hours per week, while men are logging 48.8 hours.[4] With two-thirds of married women working outside the home, this means the median husband-wife unit is putting in ninety hours a week on the job. And that's before you count the hours of domestic labor on the home front.

Such expanding work is surprising, even shocking. The reasonable prediction of the 1960s claimed that, by 1990, people would be working only twenty hours a week. Productivity gains through technology would increase wages, thereby decreasing work hours accordingly. As a result, one wage earner per family—working only four hours a day—would be sufficient to buy a house, purchase health care, put braces on the children's teeth, pay for college, marry off the daughters, and save for retirement. Even though this prediction seemed reliable at the time, it didn't happen. The prediction was leisure, but the reality is overwork.

A brief history of work shows that, throughout the nineteenth century, the workweek averaged roughly sixty hours. According to the University of Iowa's Benjamin Hunnicutt, these hours gradually declined until, in the 1920s, the forty-hour workweek firmly established itself.

Indeed, once the workweek lowered to forty hours, some companies dropped it even further. Kellogg's, for example, instituted the popular six-hour day in 1930 which lasted in some form until 1985. But mostly, the forty-hour week held. In 1980, however, contrary to predictions, work hours began to *increase*, not decrease. The slope of the increase since 1980 roughly mirrors the slope of the decrease prior to 1920.

REASONS FOR OVERWORKING

There are many reasons why work hours began to unexpectedly increase.

Economic necessity, whether real or perceived, is the most obvious reason. Many workers, trapped in low-paying, dead-end jobs, found it necessary to log longer hours just to stay even. Many others who worked middle-class jobs all their lives found wages not even keeping up with inflation. Still others were caught in the cascading circumstances of societal change: college graduates with huge educational debts; recently divorced women starting over; single mothers with mouths to feed, medicine to buy, and child care to pay.

Corporate downsizing is another contributor to the overwork syndrome. In a deregulated and increasingly competitive market, many companies have found it "necessary" to cut jobs. These companies discovered it was cheaper to pay remaining workers overtime than to pay longtime employees high salary and benefit packages. This might have enhanced corporate bottom lines, but it shredded employee creativity, morale, and any sense of company loyalty.

Increasing job insecurity is another contributor to high work hours. Those companies who ruthlessly—and visibly—put thousands of employees on the street instilled fear in the remaining work force. Such employee fear also contributes to stagnant wages, even in the face of a robust economy. Threatened workers, it seems, are wary of pressuring management for raises. This fear not only freezes wages but also causes worker hesitancy to say no when overtime is demanded of them. "Willingness to accommodate work often involves giving up weekend and vacation plans," explains work researcher Leslie A. Perlow. "You can only say no so many times."[5]

Consumptive lifestyles are yet another prominent reason for work-hour inflation. According to economist Schor, all of our productivity gains since World War II have gone toward producing and consuming more goods and services rather than more leisure. In so doing, people habituated themselves to a lifestyle of high consumption, one they now find difficult reversing. Trapped in exhausting work schedules by lifestyle excess, they also have high levels of consumer debt. This then completes the loop, as personal indebtedness is currently *the* major factor determining people's willingness to reduce hours.

An *overdeveloped work ethic* is yet another reason. While work is clearly important, nowhere in Scripture is it treated as the highest form of human endeavor. Yet today, according to Hunnicutt, work has become a modern religion, and the *mythology of work* causes people to ignore all other kinds of responsibilities. "The job resembles a secular religion," he writes, "promising personal identity, salvation, purpose and direction, community, and a way for those who believe truly and simply in 'hard work' to make sense out of the confusion of life."[6] Even though such revering of work causes significant personal, family, and spiritual problems, it is highly rewarded by our societal structure.

Viewing the workplace as home is perhaps the most disturbing reason for high work hours. In a recently observed trend, both men and women are looking for an escape from the increasingly chaotic home front, and they find it in their work. Sure, work is sometimes stressful—but anything is better than home. "We know from previous research that many men have found a haven at work," explains Hochschild, in her book *The Time Bind: When Work Becomes Home and Home Becomes Work.* "This isn't news. The news of this book is that growing numbers of working women are leery of spending more time at home, as well. They feel torn, guilty, and stressed out by their long hours at work; but they are ambivalent about cutting back on those hours."[7]

WORK OVERLOAD AND OUR FRAGILE SOCIAL CONTRACT

The enormous job creation and sustained economic growth of the past decade have handsomely rewarded movers and shakers, CEOs and CFOs, investors and stock holders. But what about the average guy in the trenches who shows up day in and day out, the gal on the line who works through her Carpal Tunnel Syndrome and wakes up every night in pain? What about that mom and dad who put in a combined ninety-hour work week while little Susie and Johnny sit in day care? In a large—and still growing—number of cases, this family is falling further behind. When they can't even afford dental care, how are they going to afford college tuition? This is the kind of frustration that worker backlash is made of, and management knows it. So do both political parties.

Since the end of World War II there has been an implicit social contract in the U.S. between labor and management that workers would get a share of the wealth they helped create. Today, it isn't happening; the opposite is. Wage inequality has returned to the level of 1940, the end of the Depression. America has the most unequal distribution of income among advanced industrialized countries. Thirty years ago the ratio of CEO salary and the lowest worker was 35 to 1. Today it is about 200 to 1.[8]

"By all odds, this should be a season of economic celebration in America. . . . But there is a gaping hole in this success story," explains *U.S. News & World Report's* David Gergen, "and that's why there is no celebration. . . . What about average American workers? Their tale is deeply troubling." Gergen goes on to point out that, compared to previous economic expansions, payrolls are growing much more slowly.[9] Perhaps wage stagnation was justified in days when productivity was flat. But lately, that has not been the case. Says Lawrence Perlman, chairman and CEO of Ceridian Corp., "There has been an extraordinary decoupling between productivity growth and compensation growth."[10]

The point is, the average family is clocking an unprecedented number of hours on the job, even to the detriment of family well-being. But they are not seeing the benefit of all their hard work and extra hours. As long as wages stay flat or decline while prices increase—which is the case for the majority of Americans—people will feel the need to put in *even more* hours. Wrong direction. My suggestion: Pay the same wage scale Jesus would pay if He owned the company.

Effects of Overwork

Even as employers continue to insist on "more," many workers are beginning to say "enough is enough." Something has to give. Signs and symptoms of overwork are readily visible and should not be ignored.

Productivity
Studies have shown that somewhere between fifty and sixty hours of work per week, productivity and efficiency begin to reverse. One study in England revealed that, at sixty hours a week, performance declined twenty-five percent. When workers are stretched too thin, fatigue and resentment surface. Yet some managers never stop pushing the limits—speeding up the line, electronically recording keystrokes, cutting down on breaks, even monitoring bathroom trips.

Illness
Overuse syndromes such as *Repetitive Strain Injury* and *Cumulative Trauma Disorder* are being called "the industrial diseases of the

Information Age." Carpal Tunnel Syndrome is one such condition reported with increasing frequency.

Sleep Disorders

With the advent of electricity and the incandescent bulb, artificial lighting stretched the day into night, thus contributing to our epidemic nationwide sleep gap. According to a survey sponsored by the National Sleep Foundation in Washington, D.C., "A staggering forty-seven percent of workers in the United States said they have trouble sleeping, two-thirds of whom think insomnia has a negative impact on their job performance, including their ability to handle job-related stress, make decisions, and solve problems."

The total annual cost of insomnia to U.S. businesses, including absenteeism, medical costs, and decreased productivity, is an estimated $100 billion. "Clearly, the high-pressure business environment of the 1990s, with its downsized work force and increased competition, is having a profound impact on the American workplace," warns Louis W. Sullivan, M.D., former U.S. Secretary of Health and Human Services.[11]

Family

The family issues are, for me, the most pressing. I am a pro-work person, and this chapter should not be taken as an anti-work treatise. But, simply stated, work must assume its rightful place, leaving at least *some* time for the family. Hunnicutt is appropriately concerned about the "hemorrhage of time" *away* from the critically important institutions of the family and church, and *toward* the institution of work.

"This is a selfish world," says ninety-eight-year-old pediatrician Leila Denmark, who still works four days a week treating children. "Parents are working their brains out to buy nice homes and cars. If we're ever going to make America better, we've got to tell [parents]—no matter how educated, how poor or how rich—to take care of [their children]. When I worked in the slums in 1918, that's where all the bad kids were because their parents didn't take care of them. Today, you find them in the suburban homes of the finest doctors and lawyers; their kids have gone bad because they have no time for them."[12]

Women

Many women feel trapped in what has been called "the stalled revolution." Decades ago they began pouring into the workplace for reasons of both personal ambition and economic necessity. Yet now, to their dismay, they are doing the math: Time spent on their outside-the-home jobs combined with time spent on their domestic work often exceeds eighty hours per week. The exhaustion is not imaginary. Many feel they have accommodated all they can accommodate. *Something* needs to be done. Families and churches should honestly confront all the issues involved and then assist in making whatever adjustments need to be made.

Men

Let me simply quote a turn-of-the-century Yiddish poem that appeared in—of all places—*The Wall Street Journal.*

> I have a son, a little son,
> A boy completely fine.
> When I see him it seems to me
> That all the world is mine.
> But seldom, seldom do I see
> My child awake and bright;
> I only see him when he sleeps;
> I'm only home at night.
> It's early when I leave for work;
> When I return it's late.
> Unknown to me is my own flesh,
> Unknown is my child's face.
> When I come home so wearily
> In the darkness after day,
> My pale wife exclaims to me:
> "You should have seen our child play."
> I stand beside his little bed,
> I look and try to hear.
> In his dream he moves his lips:
> "Why isn't Papa here?"[13]

FOUR EXAMPLES

Air Force

On a number of occasions, the Pentagon has asked me to talk about margin. As these high-performing military employees are pre-selected for stoicism, their interest in margin surprised me. But they are human and have limits just as everybody else. Take, for example, their current crisis in pilot retention.

Each pilot has undergone five million dollars worth of training. It is obviously a good thing if they reenlist when their term is finished. But currently, pilots are leaving in record numbers to take jobs in the commercial sector. Why? It is not simply that the commercial sector pays better (although it does). Workload considerations also play a role. Since the Gulf War the workload has quadrupled, while the number of pilots has been cut in half—an astounding eightfold increase in job responsibilities. Congress is attempting to address this by increasing the bonus for re-upping from $60,000 to $110,000. Yet despite this added incentive, it is predicted that until something is done about workload issues, pilots will vote with their feet and not their wings.

Engineers

The recent book *Finding Time: How Corporations, Individuals, and Families Can Benefit from New Work Practices* describes work stress among software engineers, thus highlighting issues important throughout many occupations. "Knowledge workers, like senior executives, experience immense pressure to . . . put work above all else,"[14] observes University of Michigan business professor Leslie A. Perlow, who studied a Fortune 500 company to write the book. "Engineers believe that they must be perceived as always willing to 'accommodate the demands of the work.' . . . They should be willing to do whatever is asked, not just in terms of producing output but also in terms of working whatever hours are deemed necessary to get the job done."[15] As long as nobody's getting hurt, what's the big deal? The big deal is—somebody's getting hurt.

A case in point: the Apple Computer staff designing the Newton. "The pressure to finish, exhilarating at first, eventually overwhelmed some of the young designers," explains a *New York Times* article. "After eighteen-hour days, some engineers went home and cried. Some quit. One had a breakdown and ended up in jail. One took a pistol and killed himself."[16]

Medicine

Medicine has a long, proud history of overwork. Today, however, something is different. To be sure, doctors are still putting in long hours—but the difference is, we are not bearing up very well under new pressures. The enormous changes in medicine have rocked physicians, and most are trying to regain some semblance of personal and professional equilibrium. On top of all the unprecedented structural changes, the societal reimbursement for being a doctor is lower than in times past, thus not sufficiently blunting the work stress. A medical disability company observes that many—if not most—practitioners now applying for disability "involve some impairment that the doctors could ignore as long as they were professionally motivated."[17]

This professional overwork ethic begins in medical school and intensifies in residency training. Enormous time commitments are simply expected. One week during residency I worked 128 hours—and, quite frankly, besides falling asleep in the middle of my spaghetti, I didn't think much about it. But studies reveal such overloaded schedules do indeed cause detrimental changes in medical trainees, replacing the altruistic motivation of patient service with the more primitive motive of shift survival. "For many residents, fatigue cultivates anger, resentment, and bitterness rather than kindness, compassion, or empathy," observes Michael Green, M.D., in a provocative *Annals of Internal Medicine* article.[18]

Ministry

I am deeply concerned about the stressful changes in the pastorate over the past few decades. According to one report, only one in three pastors "finishes well." Clergy burnout is so common that

Focus on the Family's H. B. London, Jr., has called the pastor "an endangered species." Denominational executive Dr. David Rambo reported that ninety percent of pastors say they are inadequately trained to cope with ministry demands, eighty percent say their ministries have had a negative effect on their families, and seventy percent have a lower self-image now than when they started in the ministry.[19] Ministry hours are long, while expectations are often conflicting—and sometimes impossible. These pressures inevitably wear on pastors, who frequently feel no permission to reveal their distress. At least twenty-two organizations exist for the sole purpose of pre- or post-burnout counseling for pastors.

In addition, the overwork associated with ministry "success" and rapid church growth can bring problems. In one instance, church attendance was swelling dramatically and the facility was bursting at the seams. Every day lives were transformed and the course of eternity changed. God was working in extraordinary ways, and the more God worked, the harder the staff worked. *If we worked seventy hours a week and touched this many lives,* they reasoned, *what would happen if we worked eighty hours, or ninety?*

There was no real structure for accountability. The staff was burning out and the core was splitting. As the pace became overwhelming, cracks began to appear in the foundation—fatigue, relational carelessness, sin. In this instance, some of the leadership got a second chance and the church went on to experience phenomenal growth. Still, the lesson is clear: Just because their field is spiritual, pastors are not immune from the stressors of work overload.

PRESCRIPTIONS FOR AVERTING WORK DREAD

If pressures at work seem to mount faster than your motivation and energy, the following prescriptions might bring balance and a new perspective.

Rx 1 *Ask the "How Much Work Is Enough" Question*
Work is so dominant in our value structure that many will not—or cannot—even bring themselves to ask the question. It seems

heretical, similar to "How much education is enough?" But it is spiritually essential that we ask these questions about every aspect of our lives. Our inability to even *think* about such issues is all the evidence we need that such thought is essential. Idolatry is often marked by subtle and unchallengeable presuppositions.

Rx 2 *Rethink the Work Ethic*

The work ethic is an important puritan remnant and part of what developed our national greatness. It is an essential component of maturity. It contributes to integrity on the job. It often results in the fundamentally important ability to pay our bills along life's way. As parents, we are pleased to see it evolve in our children. But emphasizing the importance of a work ethic should not be taken as a defense of workaholism. A work ethic is laudatory; workaholism is, by definition, intemperate. "Work is an obligation, not an obsession," explains burnout author Charles Perry, Jr.[20]

Let's rethink work for a minute. What are we really exalting? Is it work as *God* defines it, or work as *we* define it? Is it *work*, or is it *success?* The success ethic is not the same as the work ethic, and is often opposed to godliness.

A biblically authentic work ethic does not mean that work is all-important, that our ability to earn money defines our worth, that other important relationships and spiritual obligations take second place, or that people should be layered according to their professional level. And it does not mean that working seventy hours a week is more virtuous than working forty hours a week.

Rx 3 *Avoid the Extremes*

I commonly see two extremes regarding work: work avoidance and workaholism. Both are unbalanced and deviant from God's intention. I would rather a person work too much than not at all—but it's close. While not working at all can be devastating, working too hard can be likewise devastating, only in a subtler—and more socially acceptable—way. The best approach, it seems to me, is to stay in the sanctified middle. Have a solid work ethic that honors God, but be equally obedient in each of the non-work areas that God is so closely watching.

Rx 4 *Define Yourself in Terms Other Than Work*
A nearly universal psychological truth in American society, and one that has mainstream acceptance, is to obtain our identity and esteem by our work. While granting that work is a significant *part* of our lives, it is not the *essence* of our lives. This distinction is important because if we achieve our esteem through our work (defined as "gainful employment"), when we want more esteem we work more hours. But if we are already putting in fifty hours a week and feeling empty, increasing to sixty hours a week is a hollow answer. You cannot correct a wrong by doubling it.

Ultimately our identity comes from God and is not contingent on our job description or how many hours we work. At the deepest level of our spirit, life always flows smoother if we agree with God's definitions.

Rx 5 *Take Personal Responsibility*
Many people feel trapped in their work circumstances. But it is important to realize that we live in lives of our own choosing. Rather than blaming all our problems on external forces and circumstances, it is good to shine a light on our own motives. "Highly-stressed people tend to seek a place to lay blame," explained family researcher Dolores Curran. "My schedule was brutal, and I found myself complaining to whoever would listen. Finally, one good friend said gently, 'But you scheduled yourself.'"[21]

Perhaps the majority of overworked, overstressed workers today have contributed to the situation by personal expectations and lifestyle choices. No one will fix these problems for us. Often we will find options to consider if we are bold enough, creative enough, or countercultural enough. It is our life, and it is ultimately our responsibility.

Rx 6 *Be Cautious of Promotions*
Promotions are a sign of affirmation and respect, a reward for a job well done. But there can be hidden costs to these promotions: more stress, longer hours, and more travel. It is wise to gauge the consequences carefully. Write down the positives versus negatives. Discuss

them with your spouse, close friend, pastor, or accountability group. Pray. Delay the decision to allow impulsivity to wane. If the promotion seems spiritually and relationally sound, pursue it with enthusiasm. If you have significant doubts, wait.

Consider building your career more slowly than you otherwise would, leaving sufficient time to invest in family when the children are young. It is usually too late to invest in children when they are no longer children.

Rx 7 *Defend Boundaries*

It goes without saying that workers must give good work for their pay. But it also goes without saying that employers must allow workers a private life away from work. There is an important border that exists in this relationship, but one which modern technology is rapidly blurring.

Beware, for example, of the "electronic leash." When your employer offers you a pager and cell phone, think twice about the advisability of accepting such technology. "Are wireless communicators instruments of liberation, freeing people to be more mobile with their lives—or are they more like electronic leashes keeping people more plugged in to their work . . . than is necessary and healthy?" asks author David Shenk.[22] While such equipment might at times make good business sense (and usually a status symbol as well), there are other times when "unrestrained reachability" has worrisome consequences.

Rx 8 *Get Real*

A friend works for the U.S. government in a high-level job. The workforce in his department has been steadily cut, even as job demands have relentlessly increased. The office was continually asked to do more and more with less and less, a common mantra in today's environment. Finally, the top executive in this office told headquarters, "No, we will not do more and more with less and less. We will do *less and less* with *less and less.*"

I don't know how this was received. But when work demands have been pushed to the breaking point, such resistance becomes a marker of sanity.

Rx 9 *Balance Life with Work*
When bringing up the topic of balance in the workplace, be prepared for possible ballistics. One junior level manager, who himself put in seventy-hour workweeks, was reporting in a division meeting on a workplace climate survey: "I said that the people I worked with wanted a better balance between work and family. I got it right between the eyes . . . : 'Don't *ever* bring up "balance" again! I don't want to hear about it! Period! Everyone in this company has to work hard. We work hard. *They* have to work hard. That's the way it is.'"[23]

Despite this level of often predictable cultural resistance, attempts at balance are important if only because God says they are. An unexamined life will drift toward imbalance. Yet an unbalanced life will not be kind to us in the area neglected. And if God has told us to perform in a certain area—even at the "decent minimum" level—then we will not thrive if we disobey.

Listen to God's advice. Take control of the affairs of your life in each area where God has given explicit instructions and bring them into alignment with God's Word. You will discover that the Father always provides whatever time and resources we need to accomplish His will.

Rx 10 *Develop Interests Outside of Work*
When the sole meaning of our existence is found in our work, the tendency is to escalate hours on the job. But then if we are laid off or fired or disabled or retired, our whole life seems crushed. Instead, when the workday . . . or workweek . . . or work career is ended, there should be another level of meaning waiting to absorb our efforts. Develop a diversity of interests and involvements. Take up a hobby. Give yourself in service to those less fortunate. Volunteer to teach Sunday School. Befriend an international student.

Strive to make work interesting and enjoyable. But more than that—strive to make *life* interesting and enjoyable. Work is a smaller circle within the larger circle of life.

Rx 11 *Place Priority on the Family*
On one occasion I was giving a talk on parenting at a medical conference. The physician speaking before me, in a stunning display of

self-disclosure, revealed how forty years earlier, her five-year-old son came up to her and said, "Mommy, who do you think I would rather have die—you or Sparky?" This child, for no precipitating reason, said he would rather his mommy die than his dog. It was a hard story for me to follow, particularly because I know the physician who shared her heart is a genuinely compassionate person. But it certainly underscored the importance of my call to invest in our families.

"As I think back on my own life, my biggest regret is not spending more time with my kids," explains Chuck Colson. "Making family your top priority means standing against a culture where materialism and workaholism are rampant. It means realizing that you may not advance as fast in your career as some of your colleagues—at least for a few years. It means being willing to accept a lower standard of living . . . knowing you're doing the right thing for your children, giving them the emotional security they'll draw on for the rest of their lives."[24]

The way our society and our work environments are currently structured, strangely, we give the least time to those we value most. If we are wise, we will understand that success as defined by the world, isn't success. Success in God's eyes is measured by love. One day, He will push the delete button, wiping out all the time clocks, bank statements, productivity sheets, and 401K plans. All that will be left is love. And what has been true all along will suddenly be made clear.

Rx 12 *Keep Work Work and Home Home*
Arlie Hochschild has touched off a national debate with her provocative subtitle *When Work Becomes Home and Home Becomes Work.* With expanding workplace hours, home life often is neglected. As a result, the home front becomes more and more chaotic. Rather than honestly addressing this increasing level of domestic disorder, people volunteer for even *more* hours at work. They realize, of course, this will not solve their family chaos. But they are no longer interested in "solving" family problems, just escaping them.

Now that the syndrome has been explained, watch for the symptoms. Don't avoid the chaos at home—fix it.

Rx 13 *Value Mom*

Many women leave their stay-at-home job for the marketplace, not for economic reasons, but for self-esteem reasons. Whereas once outside-the-home work for women was stigmatized, now stay-at-home work is stigmatized. This has clearly compounded the work overload problem for those women who feel they are not worthwhile if they don't hold down paying jobs—but are stressed and exhausted if they do.

All people need recognition and affirmation, and studies reveal that if high value is assigned to the domestic work of motherhood, the entire family is happier. Let's remove the stigma and return the appropriate value to mom—all those NFL players can't be wrong. As the saying goes, *Every mother is a working mother.*

Rx 14 *Consider Working Fewer Hours*

"The executive who works from 7:00 A.M. to 7:00 P.M. every day," quips John Capozzi, "will be both very successful and fondly remembered by his widow's next husband."[25] By what criteria do we decide how many hours should be in our workweek? This question obviously has major implications for our time budget. Discover the optimal number of hours to assure you do not lose your passion for the work God has given you and to assure that your family can remain healthy.

If this entails fewer hours, be aware of the possible consequences of cutting back. You might experience decreased esteem from colleagues. Your production numbers will decrease, along with your income. You might discover that you are no longer playing "by the rules of the profession." But, on the other hand, in this era of flex-time, job-sharing, home offices, and telecommuting, you might also find more openness to experimenting with creative job configurations than ever before.

Rx 15 *Consider a Job Change*

If conditions at work are overly stressful and the hours are unreasonably long, consider a job change. But make any such changes carefully and prayerfully. Even though some work settings are glorious compared to others, overall it is helpful to remember that the world is a stressful place these days. The grass is not necessarily greener on the other side of the fence.

So look before you leap. Do your homework. It is also helpful to know that quitting a stressful, overloaded job is usually not a good idea until you have a replacement lined up. Otherwise you will find that the stress of accumulating debt exceeds the stress of high work hours.

Rx 16 *Cut Down the Commute*

The average commute is forty-five minutes a day, but for many it is more accurately measured in hours. Predictions indicate commuting pressure will only increase. For example, every ten seconds, a new stop sign goes up, and every thirty seconds, a new traffic light is installed.

Long, stressful commutes contribute significantly to work overload. Commuters who drive to work often show up too tired or too irritated to function effectively. If this is a problem in your work, consider going in early or late to avoid traffic. Or perhaps telecommute part of the week or even full-time. Another solution might be taking a job closer to home, or even moving closer to work.

Rx 17 *Open a Home Office*

Thirty-five million households today have a home office. This increasingly utilized strategy has much to commend it. It eliminates commuting time and obviates the need for extra vehicles, office clothes, and even childcare. Especially if you only work part-time, it can be an excellent solution. But it is not for everyone. We shouldn't be naive about how hard it is to be home and yet "unavailable" to children, spouses, and a myriad other distractions. One word of caution: For workaholics, a home office can be lethal.

Rx 18 *Job Share*

There are many more flexibility structures available today for those willing to be creative — or for those willing to ask the boss. Increasingly, two people (often women, but not exclusively) get together and work out the details of a sharing arrangement. Such job sharing allows flexibility for time off, vacation, and personal emergencies. If, for example, you suddenly need to take off three days for a funeral, the other worker might be able to fill the gap. I even know of a husband and wife, both physicians, who job share one full-time clinic position.

Rx 19 *Increase Work Flexibility Through Simplicity*

Many people overwork for one simple reason—they overspend. Overliving our income puts inordinate pressure on work hours. As long as we consume one hundred and ten percent of what we make, we will have little choice in cutting back work hours or changing to a less stressful job. Simplicity, on the other hand, brings flexibility to our work options. In this sense, consumption constrains us and simplicity frees us. Leave a margin.

Rx 20 *Bring the Kingdom of God to Bear*

Any job—even people-centered work—can become routine, automatic, and similar to an "assembly line." When this happens, the spiritual and relational dimension of work tends to disappear, replaced instead by pure productivity. When speed and overload are factored in, the assembly line-productivity-efficiency model dwarfs all other considerations.

Medicine, for example, can easily be an assembly-line profession. The recent changes in the health care field all flow in that direction. "There will be a relentless set of cost pressures for at least the next twenty years, which means those warm and fuzzy generalists will be told to see a patient every ten minutes," predicts Steven A. Schroeder, M.D., president of the Robert Wood Johnson Foundation. "They may find it's hard to be warm and fuzzy and maintain the income they'd like."[26] Such rhetoric throws down the gauntlet in compassion's face.

Long ago I decided assembly-line medicine was an unsatisfactory way to practice. Jesus' standard was to bring the kingdom of God to bear in every human interaction—and I wanted no less with every patient interaction. Of course, no physician can be super-doctor every time, and such was not my intention. But I could at least care. I could resist the modern temptation—often subtle—to dehumanize the patients. I could look into their eyes and attempt to touch their need. I could take on their burden for a minute or fifteen, listen intently, and try to lift their load.

This is what I mean by bringing the kingdom of God to bear. Everyone reading this book, no matter what your station in life or chosen career, can do the same. Whenever we come into contact with another human being—in the setting of work, or in the general setting of life—we have two choices: to relate in the kingdom of love, or to relate consistent with the commercial affairs of the world.

Don't let work overload drain the vitality of the kingdom. We are God's representatives. Let's represent His interests lovingly.

■ ■ ■ ■ ■ ■ ■

Focusing on Love

■ I don't know where we're going or how we'll get there, but when we get there we'll be there—and that's something, even if it's nothing.—J. PERELMAN

■ Martha, Martha, you are worried and upset about many things, but only one thing is needed. Mary has chosen what is better, and it will not be taken away from her. —JESUS, LUKE 10:41-42

One Friday evening during high school, our son Adam went to stay overnight at a friend's house on the lake. Their plan—quite ambitious for two teenage boys on a Saturday morning—was to get up at 4:30 A.M. and go fishing. I was initially skeptical they would be able to pull this off. Yet, because Adam was an early riser who loved fishing, it seemed that perhaps they had a chance.

Late Saturday afternoon, Adam drove up the driveway. "Did you guys get up at 4:30?" I asked.

"Not exactly," he replied. "We got up at 9:00."

"Oh," I chuckled. "You slept through the alarm, huh?"

"Not exactly," he said. "Ryan hit the snooze alarm forty-two times."

THE NEW HUMAN CONDITION

Such a Tom Sawyer-Huck Finn response to the alarm is humorous and benign. But, interestingly, we see ourselves in this mirror as well. When the overload alarms go off in our lives, we hit the snooze button. The issues are too big, the challenges too great. And besides, we're too tired. So we roll over and go back to sleep. "Hopefully," we mutter, "when it goes off next time, these problems will be gone."

But overload is not going away. Thanks to progress, it is the new human condition. And it is unavoidable.

Progress rules the Western world. It is, by now, autonomous. It has a strength and speed all its own. Our economy depends on progress, so there is no political will to shut it down. Nor, in one sense, should there be. Progress is not misbehaving. It is not evil. We are not talking about a conspiracy here. Progress is, after all, only doing what we asked it to do. We just did not realize the downside would feel quite like this.

As we have seen, progress works by always giving us *more*. Of *everything. Faster and faster.* Often at exponential rates.

Because progress isn't going to change, *we* have to change. Simply put, we have to learn how to live under these new conditions. We have to learn about the reality of human limits. We have to discover where our threshold lines are. We have to learn to *accept* our limits—no easy task when we have been so strongly programmed for growth and expansion. The rules of life are different on this side of overload, and we need to understand the practical implications for living, for working, for relationships, for faith.

Passivity is not a valid response. We must become active agents, forging the kind of response that is spiritually and relationally authentic. We need to intentionally cultivate a margin to buffer ourselves against the onslaught of overload. Many people, however, are too busy surviving each day to think deeply about it. Others are too frightened to make substantive changes. Still others have the interest and the resolve to change, but just don't know what to do.

This book has presented over 175 prescriptions for possible change in response to overload. These are suggestions, not laws. Because each person is different—different personalities, different families, different work, different expectations—each will make different choices from among these prescriptions.

But no matter who we are, there is no exemption to overload.

If we all are finite, that means we all have limits. And if we all have limits, that means we all have thresholds. And if we all have thresholds, that means it is just a matter of time before progress finds these thresholds and exceeds them. There are no exceptions to this sequence—only pretended exceptions.

CHOOSING APPROPRIATE CHANGE

Given that we all are different and have so many possible prescriptions to choose from, how do we know which options to select? If overload requires us to adjust our thinking, how do we decide which changes are most important?

There are three broad categories of change for us to consider:

>those things we *cannot* change;
>>those things we *might wish* to change; and
>>>those things we *must* change.

Those Things We Cannot Change

Many things in life will not budge, even when we get mad—for example, progress. Just because it overloads us does not mean that it will consider changing its behavior. If your boat sinks in the middle of the Pacific Ocean, just because you get mad at the saltwater does not mean it will dry up to accommodate you. Progress and the Pacific have that in common: Neither is going away.

We can't stop progress. We can't change the fact that progress rules the day. We don't have a veto. Quite honestly, I don't even think *progress* can stop progress. The adjustment to a nonprogress world would be so profound that it is virtually impossible to consider. About the only thing that would stop progress is a major economic depression or World War III. But just because we can't stop it does not take away from us the option of making individual changes to deal selectively with the untoward effects of progress.

Concerning progress, perhaps the best response is a wary coexistence. There have been thousands of benefits that progress has gifted us with, from anesthesia to abundant crops to sanitation. If we are careful, we can sort out the good from the bad. In a fallen world, it should come as no surprise that progress contains much of both.

Those Things We Might Wish to Change

Despite the things we cannot change, still we have thousands of possible options before us. Many of these options have been temporarily hidden by the strong pressures to conform to cultural expectations and live in culturally prescribed lifestyles. But even though they have been temporarily obscured does not mean they have been permanently excluded from us. If our resolve is steady enough, we can take these options back and individually become as countercultural as we wish. It helps if we are willing to be two standard deviations off the mean. And it also helps immensely if we are surrounded by like-minded people who will support our value structure.

We might, for example, wish to move to a smaller house or drive an older car. We might wish to live a somewhat simpler life, or going further, to live a radically simpler life. We might wish to have only one wage-earner in our family. We might wish to throw out fifty percent of the clutter in our homes. We might wish to wear the same pair of pants to the office for two weeks. We might wish to declare a moratorium on shopping for a month. Our choices are limited only by our imagination and our willingness to be different if sanity and godliness require it.

Most of the prescriptions offered fall into this second category—things we *might wish* to change. Let's not become legalistic about them. They are merely suggestions that will help some individuals more than others. Replacing overload with legalism is not improvement. We need equal freedom from both.

Those Things We Must Change

God still has opinions about things. Some powerful people who have opinions tend to be pushy with their opinions. In a way, so is God—not in the sense of being authoritarian, but in the sense of being right. He will let us choose whatever we want. But He is always right, which means if we choose contrary to His opinion we end up being wrong. This does not stop us from selecting that option, and often it doesn't even seem to slow us down. But being wrong carries a penalty. It is far better being right.

Those things we *must change* go beyond the realm of preference and enter the realm of Truth. When God says something that pertains to Truth, it is best if we listen. Even if we don't feel like it, we ought to pay attention and act on His advice. Even if the entire culture endorses the polar opposite, still we should listen to God. Even if it costs us everything, we should do it. God's advice always turns out to be the healthy option—even when it doesn't seem so at first. This is part of the narrow road of faith.

It is important to follow God because He really is the only One who knows where He is going. He has given us instructions and expects us to follow them. "Why do you call me Lord, Lord," asked Jesus, "and do not do what I say?"[1] If we wish to demonstrate our love for God, explained Jesus, we should do it through our obedience. If we do not obey, apparently, we do not love.[2] It is a reliable marker.

What are the things we must do? We must forgive. We must be content. We must not judge, but instead grant grace, the kind that God has granted us. We must gently tell others the reason for the hope within us (many people forget the gently part).[3]

But most of all, we must love. Not money, not things, but people. We must invest ourselves in those relationships God has blessed us with. Overload tends to block such an investment. Overload tends to obstruct the flow of love. This is why the problem of overload deserves high attention on our spiritual agenda.

OVERLOAD AND LOVE

We were put here for love. There isn't any theological dispute about it—love is the goal of the Christian life. Scripture teaches us that God is love. It teaches us that the greatest commandment is to love. It teaches us that all the commandments are summed up in the one commandment to love. It teaches us that without love, we are nothing.[4]

On that day when everything is forced through the fire of judgment, love is the only thing that will exit out the other side. It will stand alone, vindicated. It will finally and clearly be seen for the dominant, unbeatable, infinite, glorified force it has always been, just obscured for millennia by layers of fallen clutter.

We were put here to love and serve people every day of our lives. Success is nothing more than that. Anyone who says that success is more than that is not basing it on the Truth.

What does this have to do with overload? Overload sabotages love. Notice, there is no chapter on *love overload*. It isn't possible. Love is the one thing we want to see increasing at exponential rates. But the overload syndrome will not allow it.

FOCUS

The terrain outside my bus window had been baked by the desert heat. I watched with fascination as the timeless Bedouins sat guarding their sheep under the same burning, relentless sun that had parched the face of Abraham. As far as the eye could see, nothing but barrenness. I was straining to locate Mt. Nebo, where Moses was taken by God, when the Jordanian guide shattered my reverie. "All of the great religions of the world," he said, "were founded in the desert." Only one sentence, then he lapsed again into silence.

I am not sure about the historical accuracy of his statement, but there was enough provocation in it to set me back in my seat. At first, I bristled. *All you need is a sun-baked desert and a half-baked guru, and presto, a new truth is born. That's the last thing the world needs right now is another crackpot who claims to have discovered the Final Word—available now in this four-cassette volume for only $29.95.*

But God pressed down upon me, taking the oxygen away from my resistance. As I continued to look out at the desert, I went beyond offense to interest. Might it be true that the spiritual quest is intensified in the desert? Surely if you don't count sun and sand, here is no overload. One has nothing to do . . . nothing to do but think. Day after day, no change. Day after day, no distractions. Day after day, focus. Is it possible that one's thoughts might eventually climb to matters of the divine in such a setting? Abraham, Moses, David, Elijah, John the Baptist, Jesus, Paul—all spent time in the desert. Is this more than just a geographic coincidence?

If true, what is it about this desolate environment which facilitates spirituality? Is it dryness? heat? sun? barrenness? And where today can one find such a desert? In our frenzied, overloaded existence, how is it possible to focus on *anything,* let alone on God? Intel chip makers, in defending their quest for speed, report that human attention begins to wander after *one-half second!*

After years of reflection, I believe the guide's remark contains a lesson for us. The desert is waiting, poised to teach us. But Americans do not know about deserts, and furthermore, we are not interested in experiencing them. We do not know what it is like to be alone for weeks on end, clothed only with sandals and burlap, supplied with a small sack of bread and dried fish. Instead we know cities and highways, noise and lights, activities and entertainment. We know overload. We specialize in overload.

Most of us would find such a desert experience unbearable. One month and we would wilt. Our skin would shrivel and our lips would blister. We would probably hallucinate from the boredom. Despite such indisputable dreariness, the experience might yield surprising benefits.

Out of the boredom, the suffering, the barrenness, and the silence would grow a vine called *focus.* Our thoughts would begin to modulate more in the direction of a few central themes. We would stop thinking about where we left the hairspray, what time the Superbowl starts, or whether we have enough Parmesan cheese for spaghetti. We would start thinking more and more about Truth, about life and death, about existence, and about God.

THE INSUFFERABLENESS OF SUPERFICIALITY

Without focus, little of significance is accomplished. Unfortunately such is the status of our lives. The *significant* has been forced to wrestle with the *superficial.* From the start, it is a conflict *significance* should have been spared. Yet never before have so many minutes of every day gone into activities and choices which have so little to do with what it means to be alive. If we spend our overloaded workdays filling out forms in triplicate, fighting with copy machines, and fending off solicitors, we will have little chance to change the course of history. In the average lifetime, we will each spend eight months opening junk mail, one year looking for misplaced objects, and two years calling people who aren't in. What does this have to do with love?

Trivialities have always existed. But life has never held such a high percentage of superficialities as it does today. Shopping for "high-flying" basketball shoes, scanning a dozen television programs to find something good to watch, deciding between deodorant roll-on versus spray, giving the poodle a haircut, shuffling through three hundred pages of the Sunday paper, moussing hairdos, putting racing stripes on bicycles. Doesn't life have a purpose? How can we accomplish this purpose when more and more of what we do means less and less? The answer is to concentrate on the purpose, to return to it continuously.

DILUTION AND DISTRACTION

Contemporary overloading opposes focusing in at least two ways: dilution and distraction. *Dilution* occurs when too much comes too fast. A diamond on the beach is valuable until the waves crash over it. Then the diamond is nothing, sucked up by a trillion trillion tons of ocean. The gem itself is unchanged, but its value is unrecoverable because volume has displaced value.

Relationship is particularly vulnerable to dilution. We try to focus on our spouse, a child, or a friend but find that a dozen activities intervene. Soon the spouse leaves for a meeting, the child goes to soccer practice, and the friend goes to a class across town. These activities have merit, but in profusion they dilute. Relationship is replaced by experience, and even experience is watered down.

If dilution is an overload phenomenon, *distraction* is an interruption phenomenon. Interruptions are so much a part of daily living that we often do not recognize them as pathogens. Focusing requires momentum, but distraction breaks momentum's back. Focusing has to do with meditation, with contemplation. When an issue is important, we have to live with it, to dwell on it, to lock in on it. Sometimes this takes days, sometimes years. Sometimes it takes a lifetime.

Whatever the topic and whatever the duration, interruptions distract us from the important. Distractions include such noise-makers as telephones and beepers, televisions and boom boxes. Additionally, distractions are found among the many "advantages" of progress, from fashion to traffic to technology.

It may be that one task requiring our focus is parenting. But the distraction is the new car we bought which resulted in more debt and more work. Or it may be that the task is saying, "I'm sorry." Yet just when I start to speak, the pager goes off. Mr. Jones's hemorrhoids are bleeding again, and I'm needed in the E.R.

Focused or distracted: I have ridden the pendulum to both extremes (and continue to). At times focus has been sustained — although always with effort. At other times the pace of my life could best be described as furious. Perhaps this is why our family so values our time in developing countries. Life there is quite simple. While I admit that sometimes the simplicity becomes tedious, other times it is wonderfully focused. The important has time to be important without competition from the superficial.

Revisiting the desert for a moment, we now notice that essential to spiritual thinking is the ability to focus. *This* is what the desert allows. Life simplified to its basics minus dilution minus distraction. Under these conditions, momentum has a chance.

Jesus was exceptionally focused. His intent was the glory of the Father, and nothing could distract Him from it. This does not mean He did not rest. It does not mean He never enjoyed Himself. It simply means He could not be distracted.

FOLLOWING THE MAP

Although in our traveling we routinely focus on a destination, too few of us do the same in our living. Yesterday passes and tomorrow arrives, while our randomness builds only a house upon the sand. Doesn't it make sense to set our compass on the Son, to travel in His direction?

Choosing the kingdom road, we are warned, is not easy. The gate is small and the way is narrow. "Only a few find it."[5] These words ought to stir our vigilance and sharpen our focus. One would think we might tremble with fear, panicked lest Christ be correct and we fall off that narrow way. But no, Jesus always seems to be talking more to our neighbor.

Because we would be incapable of guessing in which direction Truth lies, God has agreed to help us. His Word is our manual, and without it we would have no hope. It was given not to punish us, but to free us and guide us back to Him. With its help we can rediscover what the appropriate content of our focusing ought to be—love.

GOAL-FOCUSED, GOD-FOCUSED

With this background, we are ready to consider a few final suggestions and principles which might assist us in our focusing task against the backdrop of increasing overload.

Commit to Focusing

If we do not commit, our lives will become diluted and distracted, for such is the nature of modern overload. We first must decide what it is we wish to aim for and then concentrate on it. "Run in such a way as to get the prize."[6] Each morning ask, "What is it I wish to do with this day?" Then ask, "One hundred years from now, what is it I would wish I had done with this day?" Do the latter.

Accept Responsibility

If we do not focus, life will "just happen" to us, and quickly at that. It is our own responsibility to do something about it and no one else's. "It's become clearer and clearer to me," states Mary Pipher, "that if families just let the culture happen to them, they end up fat, addicted, broke, with a house full of junk and no time."[7]

Do Not Focus on the Faults of Others

I am the problem—not my neighbor. "Let everyone sweep in front of his own door, and the whole world will be clean," observed Goethe.

Study the Scriptures

They are our only accurate Guide. Stop guessing about what the Lord has said, and let God tell you Himself. Rout out opinions and replace them with Truth.

Above All, Focus on the Glory of God and the Love of His People
These are the noblest of all endeavors, the highest of all privileges, and the sum of all existence.

Is our randomized righteousness enough to please Him? Never. But this is not bad news. If focusing is our duty, it is also our joy. If holding to the narrow road is our obedience, it is also our deliverance. Walking toward the Son is the best thing to do when you live in a storm.

ON OUR DEATHBED

Imminent death has a way of focusing our attention as nothing else. Priorities are straightened out with a jerk. Our relational failures and successes are suddenly magnified, and we wonder how all the distractions of busyness could have obscured what has now become so obvious.

While still in my training, I was called to the Intensive Care Unit bed of a dying man. He was perhaps sixty-five years old and bleeding from the neck. My job, at midnight, was to stop the hemorrhage. I talked with the nurse and glanced quickly at the chart. He was terminal, a neck tumor having eroded his carotid artery.

The scene was extraordinary. Surrounding this remarkable patriarch was his family—wife, children, and their spouses. Despite the blood, there was no hysteria. The patient was calm and alert. An oxygen mask in place, his eyes glanced lovingly from person to person around the bed. The family was gathered close, holding his hand, sober but not crying. Their eyes glistened; their mouths wore sad, affectionate smiles. They knew he was going to die and that it would probably be soon.

I put pressure on the neck wound. Not surprisingly, this caused stroke-like symptoms which seemed to reverse within a short time after I relaxed the pressure. Eventually, the bleeding slowed. I was in the room for about an hour, and then left knowing I would be back.

Later that night, they paged me STAT. The scene was similar. The patient, waning yet alert; the family still in a tender vigil. But this time, the hemorrhage couldn't be stopped. His blood pressure dropped. He looked again lovingly at his family and died.

There was something unforgettable and deeply moving about this experience. It was, of course, medically dramatic. But beyond that, I felt an awesome privilege to be in attendance as this man said good-bye. I knew few details of his life, yet it was apparent he had lived without relational regrets.

When I lie on my deathbed, I don't want to hide behind the excuse of overload. I want to be able to look my family in the eye, each one, and say, "I love you." And I want the experience of my life to confirm those words.

Overload distracts us from the true meaning of life. Overload distracts us from love. And in the end, excuses don't hold up. The choice, it turns out, has always been ours.

We want comfortable excuses. Instead, God gives us the Choice. It is in the hardest of life's choices that love is most clearly revealed. "The distresses of choice," said Auden, "are our chance to be blessed."

Notes

Introduction — *Time to Rest, Space to Heal*
1. Peggy Noonan, "You'd Cry Too If It Happened to You," *Forbes 75th Anniversary Issue*, 14 September 1992, p. 64.
2. Henri Nouwen, "Moving from Solitude to Community to Ministry," *Leadership*, Spring 1995, p. 81.

Chapter 1 — *Overload and the Reality of Human Limits*
1. Leo Tolstoy, translated by Ronald Wilks, *How Much Land Does a Man Need? and Other Stories* (New York, NY: Penguin Books, 1993).
2. 2 Corinthians 4:7.
3. Elaine N. Aron, *The Highly Sensitive Person: How to Thrive When the World Overwhelms You* (Secaucus, NJ: Birch Lane Press, 1996).

Chapter 2 — *Blame Progress*
1. Richard A. Swenson, M.D., *Margin: Restoring Emotional, Physical, Financial, and Time Reserves to Overloaded Lives* (Colorado Springs, CO: NavPress, 1992). See Part One and the Appendix: Graphs.

Chapter 3 — *Accessibility*
1. Advertisement of Digital Alliance for Enterprise Computing, *The Wall Street Journal*, 26 April 1996, p. B7.
2. Advertisement of Lucent Technologies, *The Wall Street Journal*, 17 March 1997, p. A9.
3. James M. Cerletty, M.D., "I'm Dying of Easy Accessibility," *The Journal of Family Practice*, 42 No. 4, April 1996, p. 335.
4. Lance Morrow, "Hoy! Hoy! Mushi-Mushi! Allo!," *Time*, 29 January 1990, p. 84.
5. O'Ann Steere, "E-mail Cautions: Just Because You Can E-mail a Missionary, It Doesn't Mean You Should," *Computing Today*, September/October 1997, p. 25.

6. Cerletty, p. 335.

7. Joshua Quittner, "Invasion of Privacy," *Time*, 25 August 1997, p. 30.

8. "How You're Spied On: Everyday Events That Can Make Your Life a Little Less Private," *Time*, 25 August 1997, pp. 32-33.

9. Quittner, pp. 32-33.

10. Janna Malamud Smith, *Private Matters: In Defense of the Personal Life* (Reading, MA: Addison-Wesley, 1997), p. 38.

11. Dallas Willard, *The Spirit of the Disciplines: Understanding How God Changes Lives* (New York, NY: HarperSanFrancisco, 1988), p. 101.

12. Dallas Willard, "Spiritual Disciplines," Focus on the Family 1997 Attorneys Conference, May 1997.

Chapter 4—*Activity and Commitment*

1. John Charles Cooper, *The Joy of the Plain Life* (Nashville, TN: Impact Books, 1981), p. 28.

2. David and Becky Waugh, "The Urge to Serve Beyond Our Means," *Leadership*, Winter Quarter 1984, pp. 101-105.

3. Gordon MacDonald, *Ordering Your Private World* (Nashville: Oliver-Nelson, 1985), p. 36.

4. Mildred Tengbom, "Harried Lives: If You're a Frenzied Mess, It's Time to Decide What's Really Important to You," *Focus on the Family,* October 1985, pp. 10-12.

5. Brian J. Walsh and J. Richard Middleton, quoting Augustine, *The Transforming Vision: Shaping a Christian World View* (Downers Grove, IL: InterVarsity Press, 1984), p. 99.

6. Ted W. Engstrom and R. Alec Mackenzie, quoting Charles Shedd, *Managing Your Time: Practical Guidelines on the Effective Use of Time* (Grand Rapids, MI: Zondervan, 1967), pp. 30-31.

7. Thomas R. Kelly, *A Testament of Devotion* (New York, NY: Harper & Brothers Publishers, 1941), pp. 115-116.

8. J. Grant Howard, *Balancing Life's Demands: A New Perspective on Priorities* (Portland, OR: Multnomah Press, 1983), p. 144.

9. Anne Morrow Lindbergh, *Gift from the Sea* (New York, NY: Pantheon, 1955), p. 115.

10. Jean Fleming, *Between Walden and the Whirlwind: Living the*

Christ-Centered Life (Colorado Springs, CO: NavPress, 1985), p. 40.

11. Robert Banks, *The Tyranny of Time: When 24 Hours Is Not Enough* (Downers Grove, IL: InterVarsity Press, 1983), p. 247.

12. Roy McCloughry, "Basic Stott: Candid Comments on Justice, Gender, and Judgment," *Christianity Today,* 8 January 1996, p. 25.

Chapter 5—*Change and Stress*

1. Alvin Toffler, *Future Shock* (New York, NY: Bantam Books, 1971), pp. 1-2.

2. "Longer Lives, Less Cash," *U.S. News & World Report,* 12 August 1996, p. 14.

3. Rodger Doyle, "House to House," *The Atlantic Monthly,* March 1993, p. 95.

4. James Dobson, "Americans on the Move," *Focus on the Family Bulletin,* July 1995, p. 1.

5. William Manchester, "A World Lit Only by Change," *U.S. News & World Report,* 25 October 1993, p. 6.

6. Frederic Flach, M.D., *Resilience: Discovering a New Strength at Times of Stress* (New York: NY: Fawcett Columbine, 1988), p. xv.

7. Walt Schafer, *Stress, Distress, and Growth* (Davis, CA: Responsible Action, 1978), p. 114.

8. Matthew 11:28.

9. L. D. Kubzansky, I. Kawachi, A. Spiro, III, et al., "Don't Worry: It's Bad for Your Heart," *Circulation,* 18 February 1997, pp. 818-824.

10. Matthew 6:34.

11. Corrie ten Boom, *Don't Wrestle, Just Nestle* (Old Tappan, NJ: Revell, 1971), p. 37.

12. John 16:33 (KJV).

Chapter 6—*Choice and Decision*

1. Alvin Toffler, *Future Shock* (New York, NY: Bantam Books, 1971), pp. 264 and 269.

2. Robert Kanigel, "Too Much of a Good Thing?" *The Washington Post National Weekly Edition,* 12 January 1998, p. 25.

3. Calvin Trillin, "Pride of the Pudgy," *Time,* 24 March 1997, p. 42.

4. S. D. Gaede, *Belonging: Our Need for Community in Church and Family* (Grand Rapids, MI: Zondervan, 1985), p. 101.

5. George Barna and William Paul McKay, *Vital Signs: Emerging Social Trends and the Future of American Christianity* (Westchester, IL: Crossway Books, 1984), p. 97.

6. Leonard Laster, "Analytical Overload: An Emerging Syndrome," *Hospital Practice,* 15 May 1997, p. 49.

7. Kanigel, p. 25.

8. Mimi Wilson and Mary Beth Lagerborg, *Table Talk* (Colorado Springs, CO: Focus on the Family Publishing, 1994), p. 55.

9. Gaede, pp. 90 and 148.

10. Edward Wenk, Jr., *Tradeoffs: Imperatives of Choice in a High-Tech World* (Baltimore, MD: The Johns Hopkins University Press, 1986), p. 211.

11. Larry Crabb, *Understanding People: Deep Longings for Relationship* (Grand Rapids, MI: Zondervan, 1987), p. 163.

12. "If any of you lacks wisdom, he should ask God, who gives generously to all without finding fault, and it will be given to him. But when he asks, he must believe and not doubt" (James 1:5-6).

13. "You do not have, because you do not ask God" (James 4:2).

14. Deuteronomy 30:19-20.

15. Joshua 24:15.

Chapter 7—Debt

1. Paul E. Billheimer, *Destined for the Throne: A New Look at the Bride of Christ* (Fort Washington, PA: Christian Literature Crusade, 1975), p. 53.

2. "Harper's Index," *Harper's Magazine,* March 1997, p. 13.

3. "Harper's Index," *Harper's Magazine,* June 1996, p. 13.

4. Fred Vogelstein, "Giving Credit Where Credit Is Undue," *U.S. News & World Report,* 31 March 1997, p. 52.

5. Karen Gullo and Vivian Marino, "Debt Threatens Families,

Economy," *Cedar Rapids Gazette,* 10 March 1996, p. 2F.

6. Fred R. Bleakley, quoting Maury Harris, "A 125% Solution to Card Debt Stirs Worry," *The Wall Street Journal,* 17 November 1997, p. A2.

7. Bleakley, p. A2.

8. John Capozzi, *If You Want the Rainbow . . . You Gotta Put Up with the Rain* (Fairfield, CT: JMC Industries, 1997), #66.

9. Damon Darlin, "The Newest American Entitlement," *Forbes,* 8 September 1997, p. 113.

10. Darlin, quoting Lawrence Chimerine, p. 116.

11. John deGraff, producer, *Affluenza*—Public Television Special, first aired September 1997.

12. Russ Crosson, *A Life Well Spent: The Eternal Rewards of Investing Yourself and Your Money in Your Family* (Nashville, TN: Thomas Nelson Publishers, 1994), p. 93.

13. "Do not conform any longer to the pattern of this world, but be transformed by the renewing of your mind" (Romans 12:2, NIV). "No soldier in active service entangles himself in the affairs of everyday life, so that he may please the one who enlisted him as a soldier" (2 Timothy 2:4, NASB).

14. Paul Borthwick, *101 Ways to Simplify Your Life: Practical Steps for Restoring Sanity to Your World* (Wheaton, IL: Victor Books, 1992), pp. 42-43.

15. Borthwick, pp. 73-82.

16. J. Avorn, quoting R. Fein, "Benefit and Cost Analysis in Geriatric Care," *The New England Journal of Medicine,* 310, 1984, pp. 1294-1301.

17. Russ Crosson, "Your Changing Finances in a Changing World," Focus on the Family 1997 Physicians Conference, November 1997.

Chapter 8—*Expectation*

1. Peggy Noonan, "You'd Cry Too If It Happened to You," *Forbes 75th Anniversary Issue,* 14 September 1992, p. 60.

2. Doug Trouten, "All Dressed Up," *Minnesota Christian Chronicle,* 3 April 1997, p. 2.

3. David Elkind, *The Hurried Child: Growing Up Too Fast Too*

Soon (Reading, MA: Addison-Wesley, 1981), p. 3.

4. *All-Consuming Passion: Waking Up from the American Dream*, Pamphlet by New Road Map Foundation, Seattle, WA, 1993, p. 6.

5. Gregory Beals and Leslie Kaufman, quoting David Wolfe, "The Kids Know Cool," *Newsweek*, 31 March 1997, p. 48.

6. "Perspectives," quoting Alex Molnar, *Newsweek*, 12 May 1997, p. 29.

7. Kenneth A. Myers, "Is There Really a Generation Gap?" Quoted in *Currents: Comments on Beliefs and Values in Today's Society*, July/August 1997, p. 20.

8. Randall Rothenberg, quoting Joseph Turow, "How Powerful Is Advertising?" *The Atlantic Monthly*, June 1997, p. 114.

9. John Leo, "Decadence, The Corporate Way," *U.S. News & World Report*, 28 August–4 September 1995, p. 31.

10. Chief Justice Warren Burger, "Current Quotes," *U.S. News & World Report*, 2 September 1985, p. 12.

11. George Pattison, "A Profile of Physicians in Sport: George Sheehan, M.D.," *The Main Event*, 1 No. 11, November 1986, p. 10.

12. David A. Sorensen, "Because I Can!" *Decision*, March 1996, p. 32.

13. Henri J. M. Nouwen, *Out of Solitude: Three Meditations on the Christian Life* (Notre Dame, IN: Ave Maria Press, 1974), pp. 18-19.

14. Gilbert Brim, "Losing and Winning," *Psychology Today*, September 1988, p. 52.

15. Charles Colson, "A Nation That Has Forgotten God," *Jubilee*, Summer 1996, p. 19.

16. Barbara DeGrote-Sorensen and David Allen Sorensen, *'Tis a Gift to Be Simple: Embracing the Freedom of Living with Less* (Minneapolis, MN: Augsburg, 1992), p. 19.

17. C. S. Lewis, *Mere Christianity* (Glasgow: Collins, 1952), pp. 160-161.

18. Louis McBurney, M.D., and David McCasland, "The Danger of Aiming Too High," *Leadership*, Summer Quarter 1984, pp. 30-35.

19. Tim Kimmel, *Little House on the Freeway: Help for the Hurried Home* (Portland, OR: Multnomah, 1987), pp. 159-160.
20. Lewis, p. 90.
21. Arlie Russell Hochschild, *The Time Bind: When Work Becomes Home and Home Becomes Work* (New York: Henry Holt and Company, 1997), p. 217.
22. Philippians 4:11-12; 1 Timothy 6:6-19; Hebrews 13:5.
23. A. W. Tozer, *The Pursuit of God* (Harrisburg, PA: Christian Publications, Inc., 1948), p. 112.
24. Matthew 16:24.

Chapter 9 — *Hurry and Fatigue*
1. Mortimer B. Zuckerman, "America's Silent Revolution," *U.S. News & World Report,* 18 July 1994, p. 90.
2. Peg Zaemisch, "Relishing Life Is Harder on the Run," *Dunn County News,* 26 November 1995, p. 4A.
3. Bob Benson, *"See You at the House." The Very Best of the Stories He Used to Tell* (Nashville, TN: Generoux Nelson, 1989), pp. 147-148.
4. Jacques Ellul, *The Presence of the Kingdom* (Colorado Springs, CO: Helmers & Howard, 1989), p. 56.
5. David Sharp, "So Many Lists, So Little Time," *USA Weekend,* 15-17 March 1996, p. 4.
6. Elizabeth Berg, "What's Your Hurry?" *Women's Day,* 5 February 1991, p. 54.
7. Chuck Swindoll quoted in David Kraft, "Isaiah Versus Tums," *Closer Walk-The Navigators,* July 1992, p. 37.
8. Psalm 23:2.
9. Jeremy Rifkin, *Time Wars: The Primary Conflict in Human History* (New York, NY: Simon & Schuster, 1987), pp. 223-224.
10. Mayo D. Gilson, "Redeeming the Time," *News and Reports-CMS,* March/April 1988, p. 81.
11. John Ortberg, *The Life You've Always Wanted: Spiritual Disciplines for Ordinary People* (Grand Rapids, MI: Zondervan, 1997), p. 81.
12. John M. Capozzi, *If You Want the Rainbow . . . You Gotta Put*

Up with the Rain (Fairfield, CT: JMC Industries, Inc., 1997), #8, #14, #39, and #48.

13. H. Arthur Dunn, "Biblical Concepts of Time: Helping Individuals and Families Live More Meaningfully," Doctoral Dissertation for the Talbot School of Theology, Biola University, March 1993, p. 78.

14. H. Arthur Dunn, quoting Ben Patterson, *The Grand Essentials* (Waco, TX: Word, 1987), p. 123.

15. Dolores Curran, quoting Buck Sterling, *Stress and the Healthy Family: How Healthy Families Handle the Ten Most Common Stresses* (San Francisco, CA: Harper & Row, 1987), p. 118.

16. Benson, p. 165.

17. F. W. Boreham, "The Mistress of the Margin," in *Mushrooms on the Moor* (New York, NY: Abingdon, 1915), p. 259.

18. Robert Banks, *The Tyranny of Time: When 24 Hours Is Not Enough* (Downers Grove, IL: InterVarsity Press, 1983), pp. 213-214.

19. Isaiah 40:31 (KJV).

20. H. B. London, Jr., quoting Henry Blackaby, "So Writes Dr. Luke . . . About This and That," Focus on the Family 1997 Physicians Conference, November 1997.

21. Psalm 37:7 (KJV).

Chapter 10—*Information and Education*
1. W. Auckerman, "Editor's Page," http://cjmag.co.jp/magazine/issues/1996/dec96/edlet.html

2. "Poll: Info Overload Can Hit Efficiency, Cause 'Information Fatigue Syndrome,'"quoting Dr. David Lewis, Reuter News-London, *CNN Financial Network*, 15 October 1996.

3. Richard Saul Wurman, quoting Peter Large, *Information Anxiety: What to Do When Information Doesn't Tell You What You Need to Know* (New York, NY: Bantam Books, 1990), p. 35.

4. Marc Ringel, M.D., quoting Alfred North Whitehead, *Accessing Medical Information from a Desert Island with Telephone Service* (Greeley, CO: Desert Island Press, 1996), p. vi.

5. Paul J. Fink, M.D., "Response to the Presidential Address: Is 'Biopsychosocial' the Psychiatric Shibboleth?" *American*

Journal of Psychiatry, September 1988, p. 1063.

6. David Shenk, *Data Smog: Surviving the Information Glut* (New York, NY: HarperEdge, 1997), pp. 30-31.

7. Walter Isaacson, "Man of the Year . . . Driven by the Passion of Intel's Andrew Grove," *Time*, 29 December 1997-5 January 1998, pp. 48 and 50.

8. Thomas Becker, "Thinking Small," *Newsweek*, 12 January 1998, p. 8.

9. Sam Vincent Meddis, On the Web, "Regarding Information Overload: Swings and Stars," *USA Today*, 20 August 1997.

10. 2 Timothy 3:7.

11. Elizabeth Shaw, "Is This What Life's About?" *Newsweek*, 5 May 1997, p. 22.

12. Julia King, quoting Mike Rusk, "Info Overload: A Hazard to Career," *@Computerworld*, 21 October 1996.

13. Kenneth S. Warren, M.D., quoting Lewis Branscomb, "The Evolution of Selective Biomedical Libraries and Their Use in the Developing World," *The Journal of the American Medical Association*, 257 No. 19, 15 May 1987, p. 2628.

14. Wurman, pp. 14 and 140.

15. Jeremy Campbell, *Grammatical Man: Information, Entropy, Language, and Life* (New York, NY: Simon & Schuster, 1982), pp. 222-223.

16. Wurman, pp. 53-54.

17. Ringel, p. 7.

18. L. Harold DeWolf, *A Theology of the Living Church* (New York, NY: Harper & Brothers, 1953), p. 45.

19. John 17:17.

20. 1 Corinthians 3:18-19.

Chapter 11 — *Media Overload*

1. Anne R. Carey and Suzy Parker, "Matinee Idles," *USA Today*, 10 October 1997, p. 10.

2. Ted Baehr, "Miracle on Main Street?" *Focus on the Family*, April 1995, p. 2.

3. Johnnie L. Roberts, "Hit the Eject Button," *Newsweek*, 11 August 1997, p. 46.

4. Most parents are blissfully unaware of the lyrics that sell millions each year, making these performers not only wealthy but also cultural icons to an alienated generation. Although to read such lyrics can be distressing, we will not solve the problems inherent in this ghastly phenomenon until the trend is fully understood and adopted on our national agenda. Words and themes in this genre of music include such "classics" as:

- Ice-T: cop-killing, a killer stalking President Bush, sodomizing Tipper Gore's nieces
- Geto Boys: slitting women's throats and cutting off their breasts
- Nine Inch Nails: self-loathing, sexual obsession, torture, suicide, and dismemberment
- Dr. Dre: "rat-a-tat and a tat like that / Never hesitate to put a nigga on his back"
- Marilyn Manson: nightmarish, X-rated scenarios of the occult, suicide, torture, greed
- Prince: "My sister never made love to anyone else but me . . . incest is everything it's said to be!"
- 2 Live Crew: "Nasty As They Wanna Be" album uses the "F" word 226 times, "bitch" 163 times, explicit genitalia reference 117 times, oral sex 87 times
- Judas Priest: forced oral sex at gunpoint
- Slayer: sex with the dead (necrophilia) and satanism

5. Gerald Early in *The Hungry Mind Review,* Winter 1996-1997, quoted in "Reflections," *Christianity Today,* 2 March 1998, p. 62.
6. Bob DeMoss, Workshop Presenter, *Current Thoughts and Trends* Conference, March 1997, Colorado Springs, CO.
7. Dan McGraw, "All Technology Is Local," *U.S. News & World Report,* 28 July 1997, p. 44.
8. George Gilder, "Happy Birthday Wired: It's Been a Weird Five Years," *Wired,* January 1998, p. 40.
9. Nicholas Negroponte, "The Third Shall Be First," *Wired,* January 1998, p. 96.

10. Susan Cornwell, "Dataholics," *Reuters@* (London), 9 December 1997.

11. John Leo, quoting Bill Maher, "Now Don't Interrupt!" *U.S. News & World Report,* 13 January 1997, p. 16.

12. Al Menconi, "Our Collective Soul Is Dying," *Minnesota Christian Chronicle,* 16 February 1995, p. 6.

13. Ben J. Wattenberg, *The Good News Is the Bad News Is Wrong* (New York, NY: Simon & Schuster, 1984), pp. 112 and 378.

14. Michael Medved, "Hollywood's Excuses for Sex and Violence," *Current Thoughts and Trends,* December 1995, p. 27.

15. Victor C. Strasburger, "Tuning in to Teenagers," *Newsweek,* 19 May 1997, p. 18.

16. Edward Cornish, *The Cyber Future: 92 Ways Our Lives Will Change by the Year 2025* (Bethesda, MD: World Future Society, 1996), p. 12.

17. Edna Hong, *The Nostalgic Almanac* (Minneapolis, MN: Augsburg, 1980), p. 106.

18. E. F. Schumacher, quoting James Coleman, *Good Work* (New York, NY: Harper & Row, 1979), p. 166.

19. Bob DeMoss, "Do You Know What Your Kids Are Watching?" *Focus on the Family,* August 1994, p. 3.

20. Allan Bloom, *The Closing of the American Mind: How Higher Education Has Failed Democracy and Impoverished the Souls of Today's Students* (New York, NY: Simon & Schuster, 1987), pp. 58-59.

21. Romans 12:9.

22. Craig Lambert, quoting Carrie Becker, "Literacy in High Gear: Lust for Books," *Harvard Magazine,* November/ December 1997, p. 11.

Chapter 12 — Possession

1. "Shopping Mania," quoting Thomas O'Guinn, *Signs of the Times,* March 1988, p. 6.

2. Brigid Schulte, "Living Large," *Saint Paul Pioneer Press,* 19 October 1997, p. 4A.

3. John Kenneth Galbraith, *The Affluent Society* (New York, NY: Mentor Books, 1958), p. 117.

4. Galbraith, p. 120.
5. Elaine St. James, *Simplify Your Life* (New York, NY: Hyperion, 1994), p. 11.
6. Anne H. Soukhanov, "Word Watch," *The Atlantic Monthly,* February 1993, p. 120.
7. Cynthia Crossen, quoting Liz Perle McKenna, "Americans Have It All (But All Isn't Enough)," *The Wall Street Journal,* 20 September 1996, pp. R1 and R4.
8. St. James, p. 105.
9. Romans 12:2.
10. Charles Dickens, *Bleak House* (Boston, MA: Houghton Mifflin, first published in 1853), p. 665.
11. Galbraith, pp. 117 and 125.
12. Leo Tolstoy, *War and Peace* (New York, NY: Washington Square Press, first published in 1869), pp. 430-431.

Chapter 13 — Work

1. Cindy Hall and Julie Stacey, "Quitting Time," *USA Today,* 10 February 1997, p. 1B.
2. E. F. Schumacher, quoting Thomas Aquinas, *Good Work* (New York, NY: Harper & Row, 1979), p. 118.
3. Hans J. Heine, International Editor, Institut der Deutschen Wirtschaft, *Industrie Anzeiger,* 1996, p. 7.
4. Arlie Hochschild, author of *The Time Bind,* interviewed on "The News Hour with Jim Lehrer," 15 July 1997.
5. Leslie A. Perlow, *Finding Time: How Corporations, Individuals, and Families Can Benefit from New Work Practices* (Ithaca, NY: Cornell University Press, 1997), p. 36.
6. Benjamin Kline Hunnicutt, *Kellogg's Six-Hour Day* (Philadelphia, PA: Temple University Press, 1996), p. 12.
7. Arlie Russell Hochschild, *The Time Bind: When Work Becomes Home and Home Becomes Work* (New York, NY: Henry Holt and Company, 1997), p. 246.
8. Lester Thoreau, author of *The Future of Capitalism,* interviewed on "The News Hour with Jim Lehrer," 2 September 1996.

9. David Gergen, "Squeezing American Workers," *U.S. News & World Report,* 22 January 1996, p. 68.

10. Don L. Boroughs, quoting Lawrence Perlman, "Winter of Discontent," *U.S. News & World Report,* 22 January 1996, p. 52.

11. "Insomnia and Related Problems Show Alarmingly High Rates," quoting Louis W. Sullivan, *Medical Tribune,* 17 April 1997, p. 6.

12. "Wise Woman," quoting Leila Denmark, *Physician,* September/October 1996, p. 22.

13. Rabbi Jeffrey K. Salkin, "Smash the False Gods of Careerism," *The Wall Street Journal,* 29 December 1994, p. A8.

14. Perlow, p. 3.

15. Perlow, p. 35.

16. Perlow, pp. 91-92.

17. Barbara Carton, quoting Margaret Ryan Downing, "What's Up, Doc? Stress and Counseling," *The Wall Street Journal,* 6 January 1995, p. B1.

18. Michael J. Green, M.D., "What (If Anything) Is Wrong with Residency Overwork?" *Annals of Internal Medicine,* 1 October 1995, 123 No. 7, p. 515.

19. David L. Rambo, "Come Apart Before You Fall Apart," *Briefing by the President on Matters of Interest to Colleagues in Ministry,* March 1993, p. 1.

20. Charles E. Perry, Jr., *Why Christians Burn Out* (Nashville, TN: Nelson, 1982), p. 139.

21. Dolores Curran, *Stress and the Healthy Family: How Healthy Families Handle the Ten Most Common Stresses* (San Francisco, CA: Harper & Row, 1987), p. 162.

22. David Shenk, *Data Smog: Surviving the Information Glut* (New York, NY: HarperEdge, 1997), p. 187.

23. Hochschild, pp. 70-71.

24. Charles Colson, *A Dangerous Grace* (Dallas, TX; Word, 1994), p. 198.

25. John M. Cappozi, *Why Climb the Corporate Ladder When You Can Take the Elevator?* (New York, NY: Villard Books, 1994), #374.

26. L. Tye, quoting Steven A. Schroeder, M.D., "New Doctors Become GPs," *Boston Globe,* 10 March 1997, pp. A1 and A7.

Conclusion—*Focusing on Love*
1. Luke 6:46.
2. John 14:15,21,23-24.
3. Matthew 6:15; Colossians 3:13; Hebrews 13:5; 1 Timothy 6:6-8; Matthew 7:1-5; 1 Peter 3:15.
4. 1 John 4:8; Matthew 22:36-39; Galatians 5:14; 1 Corinthians 13:2.
5. Matthew 7:14.
6. 1 Corinthians 9:24.
7. Mary Pipher in Family Therapy Networker, "The Day We Live In," *Current Thoughts and Trends,* July 1997, p. 14.

Biographical Sketch

RICHARD A. SWENSON, M.D., received his B.S. in physics Phi Beta Kappa from Denison University (1970) and his doctorate from the University of Illinois School of Medicine (1974). Following five years of private practice, in 1982 Dr. Swenson accepted a teaching position as Associate Clinical Professor with the University of Wisconsin Medical School where he taught for fifteen years. His current focus is "cultural medicine," researching the intersection of faith, health, culture, and the future.

Dr. Swenson has traveled extensively, including a year of study in Europe and medical work in developing countries. He also authored *Margin: Restoring Emotional, Physical, Financial, and Time Reserves You Need* (NavPress, 1992) and has presented widely in both national and international settings on the theme of margin, stress, overload, complexity, and societal change. A representative listing of presentations includes a wide variety of career, professional, and management groups, most major church denominations, Congress, and the Pentagon. In addition, he was an invited guest participant for the 44th Annual National Security Seminar.

Dr. Swenson and his wife, Linda, live in Menomonie, Wisconsin, with their two sons, Adam and Matthew.